THE
HEBREW BIBLE
IN ART

Page from the Kennicott Bible, Bodleian Library

THE HEBREW BIBLE IN ART

BY
JACOB LEVEEN
ASSISTANT-KEEPER
DEPARTMENT OF ORIENTAL PRINTED
BOOKS AND MSS., BRITISH MUSEUM

THE SCHWEICH LECTURES
OF THE BRITISH ACADEMY
1939

HERMON PRESS
NEW YORK

THE HEBREW BIBLE IN ART
Reprinted by Arrangement with
The British Academy
New Material © Copyright 1974
Sepher-Hermon Press, Inc. New York

LC # 74-78239
ISBN 0-87203-0458

PREFACE

THE war is responsible for the delay in the appearance of these Schweich Lectures. For the same reason the lectures were not delivered until March 1940, although originally fixed for December 1939. As I have said in the introductory chapter, this book does not claim to be more than a brief survey. It will be many years before we can expect a comprehensive treatment of the subject. While I have kept more or less to the original framework of the lectures, I have expanded the material substantially and provided it with the necessary apparatus of notes. I have tried to prune the book where possible of repetitiousness and the too frequent intrusion of the first person singular, two maladies most incident to the lecture form. I have given a considerable amount of space in proportion to the epoch-making discoveries of the synagogue frescoes at Dura-Europos, which form so vital a link in the transmission of Biblical illustration. The definitive work on these frescoes, which has been promised from Yale, has yet to appear. As I did not obtain a copy of M. du Mesnil du Buisson's book until after my own had been prepared for the press, I was only able to make a restricted use of it. Its author has not materially altered his views since the appearance of his articles in the *Revue biblique*, except in a few instances. I note that his suggestion of the 'Temple of Beth-Shemesh' for one of the frescoes is now linked with an alternative interpretation of the 'Restored Temple'. The latter seems to me a much happier solution, and is, incidentally, one which I have suggested independently. Having examined most of the wall-paintings from photographs (I have not had the advantage of seeing the originals), I have ventured to offer several interpretations of my own, with what results I leave to the verdict of scholars. I would like to draw the reader's attention particularly to the discussion of the 'obscure' Ezekiel panel, a subject which has called forth so many and such diverse solutions.

The vexed question of transliteration deserves a word or two of comment. A friendly critic has questioned my use of transliteration of familiar words and names. I ought to explain that what I have done is to adopt the system of transliteration of Hebrew and Aramaic now employed in the oriental catalogues at the British Museum. Following that system I have not tampered with names made familiar to us from the Authorized and Revised versions. It should be hardly necessary at this stage to plead for the acceptance of a scientifically devised system of transliteration for oriental languages. It is, for example, surely better to adopt a form like Muḥammad, which reproduces accurately the written Arabic, rather than to alternate between Mahomet and Mohamed or other possible variations of that name. That fine product of corporate scholarship, the *Encyclopaedia of Islam*, completed within recent years, adheres consistently to a uniform system of transliteration for Arabic, thus ensuring the elimination of unnecessary confusion. It has set an example which scholars in other Semitic languages might well follow.

A book of this kind stands or falls by its plates. I am much indebted to the generosity of the Trustees of the Schweich Fund for permitting me so many illustrations, although the *res angustae belli* have necessitated their appearance on a reduced scale. The number could easily have been extended, but I hope that the plates selected will convey to the reader a not inadequate idea of the range and character of Jewish religious art.

In these lectures I have borne in mind the art historian and the general reader, as well as the Biblical scholar. Knowing how easily the smooth progress of reading can be upset by coming across words in unfamiliar languages which are left unexplained, I have usually added the meaning of expressions in Hebrew and other oriental languages in the text at their first occurrence. I have also included a glossary at the end of the book for the reader who may have little Hebrew and less Aramaic. If this work succeeds in stimulating interest and enthusiasm (or even controversy) in a subject which has been strangely neglected, it will to some extent have justified its existence.

My obligations to those who have helped me are heavy and numerous. In the first place my thanks are due to Sir Frederic Kenyon, the Secretary of the British Academy and my former chief at the British Museum, for his friendly interest, encouragement, and helpfulness. I am also indebted to him for permission to reproduce plates from previous volumes of the Schweich Lectures. Although it traverses but a small section of my ground, I have found several useful hints and helpful suggestions in Dr. Stanley A. Cook's Schweich Lectures, *The Religion of Ancient Palestine in the Light of Archaeology*, a work of minute and faultless scholarship. For permission to reproduce other plates I am indebted to the liberality of the Trustees of the British Museum; the Director of the Gallery of Fine Arts, Yale University; the Librarian of Lambeth Palace; H.E. the Spanish Ambassador, the Duke of Alba and Berwick; Dr. H. H. E. Craster, Bodley's Librarian; David S. Sassoon, Esq.; the Librarian of the Salman Schocken Library, Jerusalem; and the Palestine Exploration Fund. I cannot praise too highly the *expertise* of Dr. John Johnson, Printer to the University, Oxford, and his brilliant staff, whose much appreciated services I gratefully record. My work, too, has been much facilitated by the kindness of Mr. W. Llewellyn Davies, the Librarian of the National Library of Wales, and by the unfailing courtesy and helpfulness of his assistants.

Finally, acting perhaps subconsciously on the Biblical aphorism והחוט המשלש לא במהרה ינתק, I have been fortunate in securing the services of three friends for the proofs. Dr. Hugo Buchthal, the Librarian of the Warburg Institute, Dr. Otto Kurz, of the same Institute, and Mr. Cyril Moss, my colleague at the British Museum, have all most generously given of their time and learning in reading and commenting on the proofs. They have also bridged for me the difficulties of working away from the Library of the British Museum by bringing to my notice recent publications and helping me in many other ways. It is in a large measure due to them that the appearance of this book has not been further delayed.

JACOB LEVEEN

August, 1942

PREFACE TO THE NEW EDITION

THE present reprint of my book, which was first published thirty years ago, in 1944, and which has long been out of print, provides me with the welcome opportunity of including a number of Addenda and Corrigenda. The list makes no claim to completeness, but embodies notes which I have made from time to time in my own copy of the book.

Interest in illuminated Hebrew manuscripts was slow in getting off the ground. Right up to the end of the nineteenth century Hebrew scholars preferred to concentrate upon the text rather than upon the art. Their aesthetic sensibility seemed little stirred in spite of the wealth of material at their disposal.

To us, for example, it is strange that one of the glories of the Bodleian Library in Oxford, the famous Kennicott Hebrew Bible, was dismissed in his catalogue by so ripe a scholar as Adolf Neubauer in a few lines, as far as its illumination was concerned.

It was only towards the end of the nineteenth century, in 1898 to be precise, that a facsimile edition of the celebrated Sarajevo Haggadah appeared in Vienna. To this landmark in Jewish art as found in Hebrew manuscripts, three notable scholars contributed. The value of this edition was particularly enriched with a contribution by that fine and many-sided scholar, David Kaufmann, on the history of illustration in Hebrew manuscripts, the first essay of its kind to appear in print.

Three decades were to pass before there appeared in Leipzig in 1927-8 another facsimile edition, that of the Darmstadt Haggadah, edited by Bruno Italiener.

Much water has flowed under bridges since the first publication of this latter book. The years which have elapsed have witnessed a remarkable acceleration of interest in Jewish art as manifested in copies of the Hebrew Bible, the Haggadah, with its wealth of representational art, the Scrolls of Esther, the prayerbooks and other works of Hebrew literature. What was previously a trickle swelled into a stream. Books and articles proliferated, as well as facsimile editions of the illuminated manuscripts themselves.

A major factor in this enhanced interest were the epoch making discoveries in a synagogue of the third century of the Christian Era of a series of wall paintings illustrating the memorable events of biblical history and the leading figures that took part in them. These frescoes owe their survival to a chance discovery made by a Captain Murphy, an officer in the British army, in the course of digging trenches in operations against the Arabs, in the ruins of the once prosperous caravan city of Dura-Europos, situated on the Euphrates frontier. By reason of the wide range of discoveries and the remarkable state of their preservation, the city has been happily named the Pompeii of the Syrian desert. I have devoted a good portion of my book to the elucidation and interpretation of these frescoes in view of their great importance.

It should be noted that the synagogue formed only a part of the vast and exciting discoveries laid bare under the direction of the master of historical method, the late Professor Michael Rostovtzeff. His book, *Dura-Europos and Its Art,* published in Oxford in 1938 brilliantly describes his achievements.

Only about half of the whole series of the synagogue frescoes was preserved. They owed their survival to the use of the synagogue as a base of military operations by the Sassanians when they inflicted their crushing defeat upon the Roman legionaries some time after 256 of the Christian Era.

We owe to chance another discovery made also in the first half of this century, which has thrown such a flood of light upon Jewish history in the first centuries of the Christian Era. I refer of course to the Dead Sea Scrolls. It was an Arab shepherd looking for a lost goat in the Judaean hills, that heralded this major discovery, whose importance can hardly be exaggerated. The shepherd, who in looking for a lost goat found so great a treasure, provides an analogue to the account in the Book of Samuel where we read that Saul, in looking for his lost asses, found a kingdom instead.

One point of intersection between these two discrete discoveries may be mentioned. While the frescoes form a vital link in the chain of transmission of Jewish iconography, antedating the hitherto earliest Hebrew illuminated manuscripts by about a thousand years, a similar time gap devides the Dead Sea Scrolls from the earliest copies of the Hebrew Bible.

To turn to the frescoes. In addition to their artistic and historical value and importance, their religious significance is further enhanced, by their forming a link, not only with Jewish but also with Christian iconography. It may now be maintained with some measure of confidence that these and similar wall paintings may have materially influenced the development of Christian art in its early stages.

The whole subject of these frescoes, in all its wide and fascinating implications, has found an admirable historian in Professor Carl H. Kraeling, who had himself participated in the excavations. He has devoted a massive volume of some 400 pages to a description of the Jewish finds in his *The Synagogue* (New Haven, Yale University Press, 1956) a book which is likely to hold the field for many a year.[1]

The frescoes still bristle with difficulties, and many problems of interpretation still remain to be solved. Nevertheless, the book is an admirable piece of scholarship, in which no problem is slurred over, and every aspect is conscientiously examined and the evidence carefully weighed.

It remains for me to thank Mr. Gross of the Sepher-Hermon Press for resuscitating this link of mine with the remote past, and giving the book a new lease of life.

JACOB LEVEEN

Cambridge, 1974

---

1. Readers may be interested in my review of the book which appeared in the Journal of Semitic Studies, Manchester University Press, England, vol. III, pp. 314-317.

ADDENDA AND CORRIGENDA

Page
12   line 22: *For* hinder *read* forbid.
30   footnote 2, line 6: *For* papears *read* appears.
35   line 31: *For* four *read* three.
42   line 20: *For* left *read* right.
—   line 26: *For* his *read* the.
56   bottom line: *For* hinder *read* forbid.
63   line 15: The presence of the *lulabh* and *ethrogh* may be taken as symbolising the Festival of *Sukkoth* (Tabernacles).
74   (no. 3): Failing clinching evidence it would perhaps be more advisable to accept the caption and treat the miniature as representing King Solomon reading the Law of Moses.
81   (no. 1): A further consideration would favour the acceptance of the original caption and treat the miniature as eschatological in character.
100   line 6: *For* a bearded angel *read* two angels, and delete the rest of the sentence.
116   line 17: *Add* (Pl. XXXIX. 2).
—   line 27: *For* (Pl. XXXIX.2) *read* (Pl. XL.1).
—   line 29: *For* (Pl. XL.1) *read* (Pl. XL.2).
—   line 34: *Delete* (Pl. XL.2).
132   line 13: *For* 1906 *read* 1926.
[141, Index III, col. 2]: *Insert between lines 23 and 24* Ashburnham Pentateuch, 64.

CONTENTS

PREFACE v
PREFACE TO THE NEW EDITION ix
ADDENDA AND CORRIGENDA xiii

I. THE HISTORICAL AND ARCHAEOLOGICAL BACKGROUND 1

Introductory, 1. Earliest reference to the art of illumination in the letter of Aristeas, 2. Corroborative evidence from the Talmūdh, 3. The Bēth-Ḥăghīrā, a family of calligraphers, 6. The question of Biblical illustration in the time of the Maccabees, 7. The attitude of the three great Semitic religions to representational art: Islām, 9. Christianity, 10. Rabbinic Judaism, 10. The earliest monuments of Jewish religious art: coins, 14. Arch of Titus, 15. Gilded glass, 17. The catacombs, 18.

II. THE WALL-PAINTINGS AT DURA-EUROPOS . 22

The earlier synagogue, 22. The later synagogue (A.D. 245), 22. The Sacrifice of Isaac, 23. The large vine, 24. The Tree of Life, 25. The Messianic paradise, 27. The new decorations, 27. David playing upon the lyre, 29. Affinities with the 'Orpheus mosaic', 29. The four 'portrait panels': Moses and the Burning Bush, 32. Moses expounding the Tōrāh, 32. Joshua and the Angel, 34. Joshua bidding the sun to stand still, 34. The interpretations of Goodenough and Rostovtzeff, 34. The other wall paintings: the Exodus, 35. The Restored Temple?, 37. The High Priest at a sacrifice, 37. The Wells of Elim, 39. The rescue of the infant Moses, 41. The anointing of David by Samuel, 41. Its affinities with a miniature in the Gregory Nazianzenus of Paris (no. 510), 42. The Esther panel, 42. Elijah reviving the widow of Zarephath's child, 43. The false prophets sacrificing to Baal, 44. Elijah sacrificing on Mount Carmel, 44. The obscure and fragmentary wall-paintings, 45. The Ezekiel frieze, 45. The obscurities of the last section, 48. The various interpretations, 48. The solution, 49. Its affinities with various Christian manuscripts, 49. The *raison d'être* of the frescoes, 51. Their relation to the Haphṭārōth, 51. *Ecclesiasticus*, 53. The service of the synagogue on the Day of Atonement, 55. The sᵉliḥāh *Mī shĕ'ānāh*, and its bearing on the frescoes, 55. The Rabbinic attitude to wall-paintings: explicitly permitted in the Talmūdh, 56. The importance of a knowledge of the Jewish background, 59. The frescoes in the church at Dura-Europos, 59. Rabbinic references to illustration of the Hebrew Bible, 59. The 'Samson and Delilah' mosaic at Malta, 60. The 'Judgement of Solomon' caricature at Pompeii, 60. The antiquity of O.T. illustration, 61. Mosaics in the ancient synagogues: Bēth-Alphā, 62; Jerash, Naʻaran, 62. Ḥammām Lif, 65. Its affinities with a (Christian?) mosaic from Carthage in the British Museum, 65.

III. THE ILLUMINATED HEBREW BIBLES OF THE EAST 66

The distinction between ritual and secular copies of the Hebrew Bible, 66. The exclusion of representational art, 67. Drawings of the vessels of the

xvi CONTENTS

Tabernacle upon a metal case of a Samaritan scroll, 67. A Hebrew Bible showing affinities with illuminated Ḳur'āns, 68. A Ḳara'ite fragment of *Exodus*, 68. Or. 9879 and 9880, 69. Or. 1467 and 2363, 70. The points of contact between the early Eastern Hebrew Bibles and the later Spanish and Portuguese Bibles, 71.

IV. THE ILLUMINATED MANUSCRIPTS OF THE WEST   72

The two classes of representational and non-representational art, 72. The French Bible and *Maḥăzōr*, Add. 11639, 72. Was the artist a Christian?, 83. Attitude of Rabbinical authority to representational art in the Middle Ages, 84. The secularization of the art of the illuminator in the thirteenth century, 85. The Schocken Pentateuch, 86. A Bible from Regensburg, 87. A lost illustrated Bible, 89. The Castilian Bible of Moses Arragel, 90. An illustrated Hebrew Psalter at Parma, 93. The German *Maḥăzōr*, Add. 22413, 94. An Italian *Maḥăzōr* at New York, 95. The Second *Haggādhāh* at Nuremberg, 97. The *Haggādhāh* of Sarajevo, 98. The Spanish *Haggādhāh*, Add. 27210, 99. The non-representational illuminated Bibles, 104. The Hebrew Bible, Codex No. 7, in the Bibliothèque Nationale, 107. The copy of the Pentateuch, Add. 15282, 107. The Farḥi Bible, 109. The Lisbon Bible, 113. The Kennicott Bible, 114.

V. CONCLUSION 118
ADDITIONAL NOTE 128
BIBLIOGRAPHY AND ABBREVIATIONS . . 129
INDEXES :
   I. General Index 136
   II. Types, Symbols, and other Subjects of Illustration 138
   III. Objects described or mentioned . . . 141
   IV. Glossary of Hebrew and Aramaic Terms . . 142

LIST OF PLATES[1] XVII

Page from Hebrew Bible (Kennicott 1, fol. 4*a*), Bodleian Library. See below, pp. 114 sqq. *Frontispiece*

I. 1–4. Coins. (G. F. Hill, *Catalogue of Greek Coins*. No. 1, pl. xx. 8 (obverse); no. 2, pl. xxiii. 11 (reverse); no. 3, pl. xxxii. 3 (obverse); no. 4, pl. xxiv. 15 (reverse).) See pp. 14 sqq.

    5. Arch of Titus. (Cohn-Wiener, *Die jüdische Kunst*, Abb. 39–40.) See p. 15.

II. 1–3. Gold Glass. (R. Wischnitzer-Bernstein, *Gestalten und Symbole der jüdischen Kunst*. No. 1, Tafel 5; no. 2, Abb. 53; no. 3, Abb. 39ᵃ.) See pp. 17 sqq.

III. Jewish Catacomb on the Via Montana, Rome. (Cohn-Wiener, l.c., Abb. 80.) See p. 19.

IV. Plan of the Synagogue frescoes, Dura-Europos. (After Rep. vi, p. 31 (339).) See pp. 23 sqq.; 34 sqq.

V. 1. Sacrifice of Isaac, Dura-Europos. (Aubert, *Gazette des Beaux-Arts*, 1938 (2ᵉ sem.), fig. 16.)

    2. Sacrifice of Isaac, Hebrew Bible (B. 30), Ambrosian Library, Milan. (From a photograph kindly lent by Dr. Otto Kurz.) See p. 23, note 4.

VI. 1. David playing on the lyre, Dura-Europos. (Du Mesnil du Buisson, *Les Peintures de la Synagogue de Doura-Europos*, pl. xxiii.) See p. 29 sq.

    2. 'Orpheus Mosaic', Jerusalem. (*PEFQS*, 1901, p. 233.) See p. 29 sq.

VII. 1. Moses and the Burning Bush, Dura-Europos. (Aubert, *Gazette des Beaux-Arts*, 1938 (2ᵉ sem.), fig. 8.) See p. 32.

    2. Moses expounding the Law, Dura-Europos. (*Gazette des Beaux-Arts*, 1938 (2ᵉ sem.), fig. 7.) See pp. 32 sqq.

VIII. 1. Joshua and the Angel, Dura-Europos. (Du Mesnil du Buisson, l.c., pl. xxi.) See pp. 33 sqq.

    2. Joshua orders the sun to stay his course, Dura-Europos. (Du Mesnil du Buisson, l.c., pl. xxiv.) See p. 34.

---

[1] With the exception of those of the coins, the illustrations are all reduced, some considerably.

LIST OF PLATES

IX. 1. The Restored Temple (?). Dura-Europos. (Du Mesnil du Buisson, l.c., pl. xxv.) See p. 36 sq.
   2. The Restored Temple, Sarajevo Haggādhāh. (Müller and von Schlosser, *Haggadah von Sarajevo*, fol. 32.) See p. 37, note 2.

X. High Priest at the Sacrifice, Dura-Europos. (*Gazette des Beaux-Arts*, 1938 (2ᵉ sem.), fig. 10.) See p. 37 sq.

XI. 1. Wells of Elim (?), Dura-Europos. (Du Mesnil du Buisson, l.c., pl. xxx.) See p. 39 sq.
   2. Wells of Elim, Sarajevo Haggādhāh. (Müller and von Schlosser, l.c., fol. 29.) See p. 39.

XII. 1. Exodus and Passage of the Israelites through the Red Sea, Dura-Europos. (Rostovtzeff, *Dura-Europos and its Art*, pl. xxiv.) See p. 35.
   2. Discovery of the Infant Moses, Dura-Europos. (Rostovtzeff, l.c., pl. xxiii.) See p. 41.

XIII. Elijah and the Widow's Son, and the Story of Esther (in Register C), Dura-Europos. (Rostovtzeff, l.c., pl. xxii.) See p. 43 sq.

XIV. Vision of Ezekiel (in Register C), Dura-Europos. (*Gazette des Beaux-Arts*, 1938 (2ᵉ sem.), fig. 5.) See pp. 45 sqq.

XV. 1. Vision of Ezekiel, gold glass, British Museum. (O. M. Dalton, *Guide*, fig. 91.) See p. 50.
   2. Vision of Ezekiel, Gregory Nazianzenus, Gr. 510, Bibliothèque Nationale. (W. Neuss, *Das Buch Ezechiel in der Kunst*, fig. 25.) See p. 50.

XVI. 1. Vision of Ezekiel (illustrating ch. xxxvii and ix. 1–6), Latin Bible (no. 3), Lambeth. See p. 49 sq.
   2. Vision of Ezekiel (illustrating ch. ix. 1–6), Castilian Bible, Casa de Alba, Madrid. (*Biblia . . . traducida del hebreo al castellano*, tomo ii, illustration facing p. 247.) See p. 50.

XVII. 'Samson and Delilah' mosaic, Malta. (Cohn-Wiener, l.c., Abb. 65.) See p. 60.

XVIII. Synagogue mosaic, Bēth-Alphā. (E. L. Sukenik, *Ancient Synagogues in Palestine and Greece*, fig. 8.) See p. 62 sq.

XIX. 1. Ark of the Covenant (?),[1] MS. syr. no. 341, Bibliothèque Nationale. (Omont, *Peintures*, etc., figs. 23–4.) See p. 64.

[1] The cross on the second illustration is a later addition.

LIST OF PLATES

XIX. 2. Ark of the Covenant (?), Ashburnham Pentateuch, Bibliothèque Nationale. (O. von Gebhardt, *The Miniatures of the Ashburnham Pentateuch*, Codex, fol. 2.) See p. 64.

XX. 1. Paradisal scene, synagogue mosaic, Ḥammām Lif. (Cohn-Wiener, l.c., Abb. 72.) See p. 65.

2. Paradisal scene (?), mosaic from Carthage, British Museum. (Dalton, l.c., fig. 49.) See p. 65.

XXI. Vessels of the Tabernacle, Pentateuch, A.D. 930, State Library, Leningrad. (Cohn-Wiener, l.c., Abb. 92.) See p. 67.

XXII. Vessels of the Tabernacle, from Case of Samaritan scroll, Gaster Library. (M. Gaster, *The Samaritans*, pl. 4.) See p. 67 sq.

XXIII. 1. Fragment of figured Māsōrāh, Hebrew Bible, State Library, Leningrad. (Cohn-Wiener, l.c., Abb. 94.) See p. 68.

2. Frontispiece, Book of Exodus, Ḳaraite MS., Or. 2540, British Museum. See p. 68 sq.

XXIV. 1. Page from Or. 9879, British Museum. (M. Gaster, *Hebrew Illuminated Bibles*, pl. 1.) See p. 69.

2. Page from Or. 9880, British Museum. (Gaster, l.c., pl. II.) See pp. 69 sqq.

XXV. 1. Aaron lighting the Menōrāh, Add. 11639, British Museum. See p. 74 (no. 1).

2. The Sacrifice of Isaac, Add. 11639. See p. 79 (no. 11).

XXVI. 1. Destruction of Sodom and Gomorra, Add. 11639. See p. 75 (no. 7).

2. The Cherubim over the Mercy Seat, Add. 11639. See p. 79 (no. 12).

XXVII. 1. The High Priest and the Urim and Thummim, Add. 11639. See p. 79 sq. (no. 14).

2. The Triumph of Mordecai, Add. 11639. See p. 80 (no. 19).

XXVIII. 1. The Destruction of Sodom (?), Add. 11639. See p. 81 (no. 1).

2. Moses cleaving the Red Sea with his rod, Add. 11639. See p. 82 (no. 3).

LIST OF PLATES

XXIX. Frontispiece, Hebrew Pentateuch, &c., Salman (Schocken) Library, Jerusalem. (Sotheby & Co., Catalogue of Sale, July 20–2, 1936, lot 25.) See p. 86 sq.

XXX. 1. Death of Moses, Castilian Bible, Casa de Alba, Madrid. (*Biblia . . . traducida*, &c., tomo i, illustration facing p. 463.) See p. 91.
2. Episodes in the Story of Esther, Castilian Bible. (*Biblia . . . traducida*, &c., tomo ii, illustration facing p. 565.) See p. 92.

XXXI. 1–2. Miniatures from the Haggādhāh, Add. 27210, British Museum. See p. 102 sq.

XXXII. 1–2. Miniatures from the same Haggādhāh. See p. 103 sq.

XXXIII. Frontispiece to Book of Numbers, Add. 15282, British Museum. See p. 108.

XXXIV. 1. Maze leading to (and from) Jericho, Farḥī Bible (p. 22), Library of D. S. Sassoon, Esq., London. See p. 110.
2. Tents of Jacob and his wives, Farḥī Bible (p. 25). See p. 111.

XXXV. 1. The Mᵉnōrāh, Farḥī Bible (p. 182). See p. 111.
2. Musical instruments of the Levites, Farḥī Bible (p. 186). See p. 111 sq.

XXXVI. 1. Tables of the Law, &c., Farḥī Bible (p. 187). See p. 112.
2. Arabesque, Farḥī Bible (p. 64). See p. 112.

XXXVII. Page from Lisbon Bible, Or. 2626 (fol. 8*a*). See p. 113.

XXXVIII. Another page from the same Bible, Or. 2626 (fol. 182*a*). See p. 113 sq.

XXXIX. 1. Page from Hebrew Bible, Kennicott 1 (fol. 7*a*), Bodleian Library, Oxford. See p. 116.
2. Another page from the same Bible (fol. 9*b*). See p. 116.

XL. 1. King David, Kennicott 1 (fol. 180*a*). See p. 116.
2. Jonah and the Whale, Kennicott 1 (fol. 305*a*). See p. 116.

XLI. 1. 'Shield of David', Kennicott 1 (fol. 122*b*). See p. 116 sq.
2. Arabesque, Kennicott 1 (fol. 352*b*). See p. 116.

CHAPTER I
THE HISTORICAL AND ARCHAEOLOGICAL BACKGROUND

THE subject of these Lectures is the Hebrew Bible in Art. In contrast to so many other aspects of Biblical literature, whose ever-growing volume induces such a feeling of impotence and despair, the study of the Hebrew Bible in art, by which I mean the study of illuminated and illustrated manuscripts of the Old Testament in the original tongue, has suffered from unmerited neglect. How great that neglect has been can be gauged from the fact that a brief survey of illuminated Hebrew Bibles by the late David Kaufmann, published in Vienna in 1898, still remains, after all these years, the only thing of its kind.[1] Three years afterwards, in 1901, the late Dr. Gaster, whose scholarship covered so wide a range, published a lecture upon two early Hebrew illuminated Bibles, which then formed part of his collection, but which have since been acquired by the British Museum.[2] Unfortunately, the lead given by these two scholars was not seriously followed up until the last fifteen years or so, when Dr. Zofja Ameisenowa and Mrs. Wischnitzer-Bernstein began to publish from time to time articles upon several Hebrew illuminated Bibles, as well as other writings bearing on the subject.[3] Valuable and stimulating as this work has been, it suffers to some extent from an inadequate correlation of the artistic material with the Rabbinic background, owing to a lack of first-hand acquaintance with the latter. The subject may therefore still be said to be in its infancy. These lectures do not claim to be more than prolegomena and in the nature of a preliminary survey of the material.

[1] *Zur Geschichte der jüdischen Handschriftenillustration.* It appears as an appendix in *Die Haggadah von Sarajevo*, Vienna, 1898 (pp. 253–311).
[2] *Hebrew Illuminated Bibles of the IXth and Xth Centuries*, London, 1901.
[3] The reader will find a selection from the books and articles by these authors noted in the *Bibliography*.

To embark at present upon a comprehensive study of the subject, when not even an inventory of Hebrew illuminated Bibles exists, would indeed be a foolhardy undertaking. It will require the labour of many people, historians of art as well as Hebraists and Rabbinic scholars, before the material can be adequately organized and its relation to Christian and Muslim art correctly determined. The subject has suffered to a large extent from falling between two stools, the historian of art being deterred by his ignorance of Hebrew and the Biblical and Rabbinic background, and the Hebrew scholar by his unfamiliarity with art and its history.

A wide gap extending over many centuries separates the literary and archaeological evidence bearing upon our subject from the earliest extant examples of illuminated Hebrew Bibles. In contrast to the Christians, the Jews cannot show such early copies of illuminated Bibles as the Cotton Genesis, the Quedlinburg fragments, or the Vienna Genesis. On the other hand, it is noteworthy that the first recorded reference anywhere to gold illumination in manuscripts comes from a Jewish source. It appears in the so-called Letter of Aristeas. This celebrated document purports to be written by a Greek courtier of the name of Aristeas in the time of Ptolemy Philadelphus (285–247 B.C.), but—it is generally agreed—was actually composed by a Jew of Alexandria with the object of glorifying his people and religion. Scholars have disputed the date of the letter, but moderate opinion places it somewhere in the first half of the second century B.C. Although not free from palpable errors and absurdities, the importance of this earliest account of the first Greek translation of the Pentateuch has been increasingly recognized since the middle of the nineteenth century. The passage alluding to gold illumination occurs in § 176 of the letter. In describing the reception of the translators at Alexandria, the author says:

'(176) And when they entered with the gifts which had been sent and the precious parchments, whereon was inscribed the law in gold in the Jewish characters, the material being wonderfully preserved, and the joining of the leaves being rendered imperceptible, the king when he saw the men, made enquiry concerning the books. (177) And when they had taken the rolls out of their coverings and unrolled the leaves, the king after pausing for a long while and making obeisance some seven times, said, "I thank you, friends, and him that sent you still more, but most of all do I thank God, whose oracles these are".[1]

The statement that the scrolls were written in letters of gold is repeated both by Philo and Josephus, neither of whom questions its veracity. It has been left for an eminent Septuagint scholar of our own times to challenge its authenticity. 'This story', asserts Swete bluntly, 'may be dismissed at once, it belongs to the picturesque setting of romance.'[2] Unfortunately, Swete did not bring forward any arguments in support of his contention, an omission which seriously weakens the force of his summary rejection. Moreover, Swete was unacquainted with the Rabbinic parallels to this tradition, a knowledge of which might have tempered the severity of his judgement. The Talmūdh contains no less than three references to gold writing. The earliest of these occurs in the tractate *Shabbāth* of the Babylonian Talmūdh.[3] We are there told, on the authority of a *Bāraithā*,[4] that any scroll of the law with the names of God found written in gold must be 'hidden', that is to say, it must be withdrawn from use. The inclusion of this statement in a *Bāraithā* enables us to assign a date to it ranging between A.D. 10 and 220. It is to be regretted that we do not possess other evidence by which we could reduce this wide margin of time. But allowing even the latest possible date, we are still a long way off from the time when illuminated Bibles had become the

---

[1] I quote from the translation of St. John Thackeray. See *JQR* xv (1903), 370.
[2] *An Introduction to the Old Testament in Greek*, Cambridge, 1914, p. 22.
[3] 103*b*.
[4] A *Bāraithā* is a Rabbinic pronouncement which, while made by a Tannā, does not actually form part of the Mishnāh.

fashion amongst Christians.[1] For, as you may remember, it was not until the fourth century that these *éditions de luxe* of the Bible began to flourish in such profusion that they shocked the austerity of Jerome and called forth his stern condemnation. Nor can it be said that this *Bāraithā* just echoes Aristeas, for the form in which the tradition here appears is materially different, the emphasis being laid upon the use of gold for the names of God only. The same emphasis is to be observed in the two remaining Talmūdhic references, which are to be found in the two recensions of *Sōph ͤrīm* respectively known as I and II. The tractate, which concerns itself with minute instructions to scribes (*sōph ͤrīm*) for the copying of Biblical texts, particularly scrolls of the law, is one of the so-called minor tractates of the Talmūdh. The first of these passages says:

'[The Tōrāh] must not be written in gold. There was a case of a copy of the Tōrāh belonging to Alexandrians, where the names of God were all written in gold. The matter was brought before the sages, who ordered that the copy be hidden.'[2]

The third and last quotation, which repeats the passage I have just quoted in a slightly different form, declares:

'It is forbidden to read a scroll of the law where the names of God are suspended (that is to say, written from the top of the line) in gold. There was a case of a scroll belonging to Alexandrians where the names of God were suspended in gold. The matter was brought before the sages, who prohibited its use.'[3]

---

[1] 'We do not know how soon was introduced the extravagant practice of producing sumptuous volumes written in gold or silver upon purple-stained vellum. It was a manuscript of this description which Julius Capitolinus, early in the fourth century, put into the possession of the younger Maximin.' (E. Maunde Thompson, *Greek and Latin Palaeography*, Clarendon Press, Oxford, 1912, p. 32.)

[2] *I Sōph ͤrīm* I. 8. See the edition of M. Higger, *New York*, 1937. I read with Blau אלכסנדריים (Alexandrians) in preference to אלכסנדרוס (Alexander), which does not make such good sense. To read in this passage a reference to Alexander (the Great) would be straining probability. See Blau, *Studien zum althebräischen Buchwesen*, p. 162, note 1.

[3] *II Sōph ͤrīm* I. 7. Here again, the emendation אלכסנדריים (Alexandrians) should be adopted. See Blau, l.c., note 2.

ARCHAEOLOGICAL BACKGROUND 5

These last two passages are, of course, much later, but they serve to reinforce the earlier reference in *Shabbāth*. It is remarkable that all the three passages refer to scrolls of the law, where only the names of God have been picked out in gold, although the passage in *Sōpherīm* I also contains a general prohibition against its use in manuscripts.[1] The emphasis on the restricted use of gold for the names of God only has led the late Dr. Israel Abrahams[2] to accept this modified version of the tradition and to reject Aristeas. But whether Aristeas or the Talmūdh is the repository of the true tradition is a question which requires further investigation. It is possible that both traditions are right. In the face of the evidence provided both by Aristeas and the Talmūdh, it would be rash to dismiss the existence of gold illumination amongst the Jews in early times as a mere figment of the imagination. The case for summary rejection is still further weakened when we consider how strongly ingrained was the love for gold ornament among the ancient Israelites. We see it, for example, manifested from the earliest days in the Biblical description of the vessels of the Tabernacle, and of King Solomon's Temple and Palace. In later times the gold phylactery cases, the gold bands with which the Jews of Jerusalem tied their palm branches, the gold glass found in the Jewish catacombs of Rome, all attest the peculiar esteem in which this precious metal was held and its wide use in the making of cult and ritual objects. Another point to consider is that as the Jews employed vellum long before it came into general use in the Graeco-Roman world, they would not be slow to realize the pre-eminent merits of this material for the purposes of illumination. Later, it is true, the Rabbis extended their ban to the use of gold illumination in scrolls of the law and in other ritual objects.[3] Although the ostensible reason

[1] Copies of the Christian Bibles of later times show a similar practice amongst Christians of embellishing the name of God in gold and silver.
[2] See *JQR* xiv (1902), 340.
[3] For a reference to gold and silver illumination in the Midhrāsh, see Blau, op. cit., p. 159.

given was that the selection of God's name for gold writing would distract the reader from his devotion, it is equally likely that the Rabbis were animated by the same dislike of seeing luxury associated with the Scriptures as characterized the Christian Fathers. If it be asked why no early Jewish examples of the illuminator's art have survived into present times, the answer is twofold. In the first place, the argument that because a thing has not survived it has never existed is being continually refuted by the discoveries of archaeology. Secondly, the very effectiveness of the Rabbinical injunction against the use of gold illumination may have caused the disappearance of copies so embellished, although the possibility of such specimens ever coming to light should not be ruled out.

The danger of rushing to conclusions is illustrated by an article which appeared a few years ago in the *Jewish Quarterly Review*.[1] The author boldly headed it 'A Family of Illuminators in the Time of the Second Temple', although nowhere in the passages cited from the authorities is there a single reference to the art of illumination. The family alluded to is the well-known Beth Ḥaghrā or Ḥăghīrā, which carried on its profession from father to son for many generations. In fact, a passage in the Jerusalem Talmūdh asserts that this family was able to trace back its lineage to a similar family of scribes mentioned in the first Book of Chronicles (ii. 55) through an ancestor of the name of Rechab. Interesting is the way in which this family is described. They are not just called scribes (the Hebrew word for which is *sōphēr*, plural *sōpheᵉrīm*), but *kathbānīm ummānīm*, which may be rendered as artist-scribes or calligraphers. On the strength of this description, the author to whom credit is due for assembling the scattered references to this family of calligraphers, proclaims them illuminators. It would be tempting to read this meaning into the words *kathbānīm ūmānīm*, but such an inference is not justified by the evidence available. We do learn, however, from these

[1] P. Romanoff, *JQR* n.s. xxvi. 29–35.

ARCHAEOLOGICAL BACKGROUND

references in the Jerusalem Talmūdh that there existed a special class of calligraphers in the time of the Second Temple in the last century of its existence, side by side with the ordinary scribes. But we cannot yet answer the question as to what their art consisted of, whether they practised gold writing of the kind mentioned in Aristeas or whether their calligraphy was done with ink only. As the Bēth Ḥăghīrā were a family of Rabbis and scholars as well as calligraphers, it is difficult to believe that they would have cultivated the art of illumination in defiance of the Rabbinical ban, unless it is presumed that such a ban was issued later. It must be remembered, too, in this connexion, that the illuminated copies of the Tōrāh which the Rabbis ordered to be 'hidden' came from Alexandria and not from Palestine.

Allied to the question of illumination in ancient Hebrew Bibles is that of illustration. An obscure verse in 1 Maccabees iii. 48 has been laid under tribute in support of the existence of such illustrations from early times. The verse in the Greek *textus receptus* reads as follows:

καὶ ἐξεπέτασαν τὸ βιβλίον τοῦ νομοῦ, περὶ ὧν ἐξηρεύνων τὰ ἔθνη τὰ ὁμοιώματα τῶν εἰδώλων αὐτῶν

which the Revised Version bravely renders:

'And they [i.e. Judas Maccabaeus and his followers] laid open the book of the law, concerning which the Gentiles were wont to inquire, seeking the likenesses of their idols.'

In spite of the heroic efforts of the translators, the sentence is not very intelligible as it stands. In the first place the words περὶ ὧν introducing the relative clause are difficult to construe unless we take them in the sense of 'concerning copies of which'. But such a loose construction would hardly satisfy the Greek purist. The sentence, too, hangs in the air. It is here that the minuscule manuscripts of the Septuagint come to our rescue. For some of them, including the famous no. 55, expand the verse by the addition of τοῦ ἐπιγράφειν ἐπ' αὐτῶν after τὰ ἔθνη. With the help of this welcome reading, without which the verse is almost meaningless, we are able to arrive at a better comprehension of its contents.[1] In its expanded form the sentence might now be translated:

'And they laid open the book of the law, for copies of which the Gentiles were making a search, in order to draw upon them the likenesses of their idols.'

By committing this act of sacrilege the Gentiles would outrage the deepest religious feelings of the Jewish people as well as render such copies of the law unfit for ritual use. It could not have been the rarity of the material which caused the Gentiles to seek for copies of the Tōrāh. For we know that after Attalus I parchment was chiefly employed in Syria and Pergamene Asia Minor, whereas papyrus still monopolized the rest of the Hellenistic and Roman world. Perhaps they used the margins of these scrolls upon which to execute their pictures, or the back of the vellum after smoothing down the rough surface, the material being so suitable for the purpose. Some scholars have ventured to read into this verse a confirmation of the existence of illustrated Jewish scrolls of the law, in emulation of which the Gentiles made pictures of their own. Such an inference does not, however, seem to be justified.[2]

Having surveyed briefly the somewhat arid questions of literary origins, *loci classici*, and so forth, where a mass of hypothesis and conjecture is embedded in a nucleus of fact, we can now turn our attention to the more concrete aspects of the subject as represented by the historical monuments which have survived from the past, or have been lately brought to light by excavations. For it is from these that

[1] Other minuscule manuscripts noted by Holmes and Parsons are 74 and 243.

[2] See Robert Eisler, in *Aréthuse*, fasc. 26, p. 30 f. Eisler draws attention to the reading of the minuscule manuscripts (l.c., pp. 36–7, note 13). He is, however, mistaken in thinking that he is the first to have seen in 1 Maccabees iii. 48 a reference to the existence of illuminated scrolls of the law among the Jews. See I. Abrahams in *JQR* xiv (1902), 341.

ARCHAEOLOGICAL BACKGROUND

we shall be enabled to trace the gradual growth and evolution of picture-cycles and motifs derived from the Hebrew Bible and other sources, and their subsequent diffusion in the pages of illuminated Hebrew manuscripts. But before doing so it might be well to discuss briefly the attitude of Rabbinical Judaism towards art, more particularly representational art, and, at the same time, to clear away certain misconceptions upon the subject which have persisted obstinately in the face of the clearest evidence to the contrary.

The contrast between the three great Semitic religions, Judaism, Christianity, and Islam in their respective attitudes to representational art is highly instructive. Of the three, Islam is the most rigidly uncompromising in its hostility. Muslim theologians are adamant in their refusal to permit either painting or sculpture.[1] That this ban was sometimes not observed was shown conclusively by the late Sir Thomas Arnold in his Schweich Lectures on the 'Old and New Testaments in Muslim Religious Art'. That does

[1] The Muslim prohibition against representational art derives not from a text in the Ḳur'ān but from one of the 'traditions' (*ḥadīth*) according to which those most severely punished would be the *muṣawwirūn* (fashioners of likenesses). While this prohibition was rigorously enforced in the mosque, secular buildings occasionally defied it. The bath and pleasure-house of the Umayyads discovered at Ḳuṣair 'Amrah in Transjordan by Alois Musil contains the earliest illustrations of Muslim representational art extant. The mural paintings were probably executed by Christian artists. Included in these frescoes are pictures of six Royal personages, among them the caliph himself (according to Musil, Walīd II (A.D. 743–4), according to others, Walīd I (705–15)), and his enemy Roderic, the last Visigoth King of Spain. It is significant that the Muslim manual of Muḥammadan law, *Ma'ālim al-Ḳurba*, expressly forbids paintings even on the walls of bath houses (*ḥammām*). See the edition by R. Levy, in the Gibb Series, pp. 190, 289. Muḥammad's suspicion of artists possibly arose from his regarding them as endowed with supernatural powers, thus exposing themselves to the charge of competing with God's creative powers. See T. W. Arnold, *Old and New Testaments in Muslim Religious Art*, London, 1932, p. 2. For an authoritative account of the Muslim attitude to painting and for a description of the wall-paintings at Ḳuṣair 'Amrah, see now P. K. Hitti, *History of the Arabs* (2nd ed.), London, 1940, pp. 268–71.

not mean that there was ever a relaxation of the ban by Islam, but that it was in certain individual cases deliberately defied or ignored. Far different was the attitude of the Christian Church. In spite of constantly recurring opposition, of which the diatribes of Tertullian, Jerome, and Eusebius, the thirty-sixth Canon of the Synod of Elvira and the fanatical outbursts of the iconoclasts are typical examples, it may be said, broadly speaking, that the Church, both Eastern and Western, not only finally permitted painting and sculpture as well as other forms of the plastic arts, but even encouraged and patronized them. For it realized quite early in its career that it was more prudent to impress the artist into its service *ad majorem Dei gloriam* than to suppress him.

Rabbinical Judaism may be described on the whole as steering a middle course between the inflexible hostility of Islam and the relatively benign and tolerant attitude of Christianity. To begin with sculpture first, the Rabbis were at no time completely reconciled to its use in the synagogue. The general rule which Rabbinical Judaism formulated, and to which the practice of the Greek Church was curiously analogous, was that all representational art, where the object portrayed projected from the surface of the material, was forbidden. Such a ban included therefore not only statuary but embossed work, bas-reliefs, and coins and medals.[1] In actual practice, the Rabbis showed a great deal of latitude in applying this law. It is only in this way that we can explain the presence of the famous lion carved in basalt found in the ancient synagogue of Chorazin, as well as other examples elsewhere. The lion, it is true, enjoyed a privileged position, owing to his symbolical identification in the peoples' mind with Judah and Israel.[2]

---

[1] For the Rabbinical attitude to images, see now E. Bevan, *Holy Images*, London, 1940. See also E. L. Sukenik, *Ancient Synagogues in Palestine and Greece*, pp. 61-7.

[2] Some Rabbinical authorities went as far as to permit the fashioning of a lion to help in curing sickness. See the quotation from the *Shiltē*

A sculptured representation of this quasi-heraldic beast could therefore no longer be regarded as a potential object of idolatry. In fact, in later times the lion carved in wood appears frequently upon shrines of the law. That sculpture was not solely confined to representations of the lion is attested by the remains of the friezes in the ancient synagogues of Palestine and bordering countries, where figures of all kinds, human, mythical, and animal are depicted. In many cases these figures have been defaced, showing how obstinately the prejudice against graven images persisted, even when the danger of idolatry had become remote. But sculpture never really became acclimatized in the synagogue. Its close association, first with pagan worship, and later with the Church, militated against its free employment in the Jewish house of prayer. With the stern Biblical prohibition of idols and images always in their thoughts, the Rabbis were hardly likely to welcome effusively the introduction of such an art into the synagogue, although they were reluctantly compelled to make occasional concessions to the spirit of the times.[1]

hag-Gibbōrīm of Joshua Boaz, in the illuminating article 'Art in the Synagogue', by D. Kaufmann, *JQR* ix (1896–7), p. 260. The subject is touched upon by E. Bevan in his *Holy Images*, London, 1940, pp. 62–3.

[1] We have it on the authority of the Babylonian Talmūdh that the Second Temple contained no plastic copies of the cherubim, but only painted images of them. See *Yōmā*, 54a. The statement reads: אחא בר יעקב אמר לעולם במקדש שני וכרובים דצורתא הוו קיימי (Ahā, the son of Jacob, said, 'The cherubim in the Second Temple were painted'). Josephus reflects the current dislike of images of living creatures not only in places like the Temple of Herod (*Arch.* xvii, § 151), but even in private buildings like the palace of Herod Antipas (l.c. iii, §§ 113, 126). That the Rabbinical interdiction against plastic images was somewhat relaxed in the succeeding centuries is made clear by the remains of the ancient synagogues of Palestine and the bordering countries (2nd to 4th century A.D.). In more modern times we see once again a more liberal attitude adopted for a time towards plastic representation. We not only meet with the pelican, the salamander, and other animals (including, of course, the lion) executed in bas-relief upon tombstones, but also with scenes from the Hebrew Bible. The famous

In their attitude to two-dimensional art the Rabbis were far more liberal. The Jerusalem Talmūdh preserves for us two passages, both in ʿĀbhōdhāh Zārāh, where we find painting and mosaic respectively permitted.¹ 'In the days of Rabbi Jochanan', says the Talmūdh, 'men began to paint pictures on the walls, and he did not hinder them.' This Rabbi—his full name was Jochanan bar Nappāḥā—was the famous Palestinian Āmōrā of the second generation, who was born towards the close of the second century and died in A.D. 279. He is thus contemporary with the synagogue at Dura, where the famous wall-paintings have been discovered in recent times. I will deal with these later. Here I only wish to say that it is quite clear from the passage which I have just quoted, that the wall-paintings of Dura are not to be considered as an isolated and possibly unique example due to the liberal attitude adopted by the local heads of the community, but rather as the hitherto sole surviving specimen of a form of art common to many synagogues of the time. The other passage in ʿĀbhōdhāh Zārāh is a similarly worded pronouncement in favour of mosaics.² 'In the days of Rabbi Abbūn', it says, 'men began to make designs on mosaics, and he did not hinder them.' As Abbūn lived in the first half of the fourth century, we are here provided, as in the case of mural paintings, with a date for

tombstone of Rachel Senior Teixeira (died 6 March 1716), a fine example of the art of the monumental mason, reproduces in relief the death at childbirth of Rachel, the wife of the patriarch Jacob. (The person commemorated upon the tombstone died in similar circumstances.) Other subjects treated on tombstones are the Sacrifice of Isaac, Jacob's Dream, and God (who is actually represented) appearing before the infant Samuel. For illustrations and descriptions of such tombstones, see D. Henriques de Castro, *Keur van Grafsteenen*, Leyden, 1883.

¹ 48d.
² This passage, which also belongs to the same place in ʿĀbhōdhāh Zārāh, 48d, is not to be found in the usual recensions. It was retrieved from a Geniza fragment in the State Library of Leningrad by J. N. Epstein. See his article in the Hebrew periodical *Tarbīṣ*, iii. 15 ff.; also Sukenik's *Ancient Synagogues of Palestine and Greece*, p. 27.

ARCHAEOLOGICAL BACKGROUND

the introduction of mosaics into the synagogue. From the wording of both these pronouncements it is evident that the Rabbis only gave their consent reluctantly to these innovations. That the path of toleration did not always run smooth is illustrated by the well-known passage in the tractate *'Ăbhōdhāh Zārāh* of the Babylonian Talmūdh, in which the Rabbis seek to justify Rabban Gamaliel's conduct in having upon the wall of his upper chamber a picture or chart showing the various phases of the moon. His purpose in doing so was to elicit more effectively from inexpert witnesses the form of the moon as seen by them, as it was most important to get right the exact time of the appearance of the New Moon.[1] Highly instructive and illuminating as this discussion is, I can only deal with one of the excuses offered by the Rabbis in extenuation of Gamaliel's apparent breach of the law. They asserted that as he had used this picture or chart in the presence of witnesses, he could not lay himself open to the charge of idolatry, for such worship would have taken place in private. To such dialectic exercises were the Rabbis reduced in order to reconcile the conflicting claims of representational art and ritual law.

Generally speaking it may be said that even when the danger of idolatry had ceased to be real, the Rabbis regarded representational art as a form of distraction for the congregation, leading them away from their religious devotion, the only proper business of man's existence. Maimonides himself relates, in a responsum, that he was in the habit of closing his eyes in order that his attention might not be diverted from prayer, whenever he found himself in the synagogue facing a wall hung with textiles embroidered with pictorial representations. The responsa literature of the Middle Ages and later times provides many illustrations of the fluctuating struggle between the advocates of representa-

---

[1] *'Ăbhōdhāh Zārāh* (T.B.), 24a–b, duplicate in T.B. *Rō'sh hash-Shānāh* 42b–43b. The reference is to Gamaliel II, the Patriarch, who flourished at the end of the first and beginning of the second century and lived at Jabneh. He was a Tannā of the second generation.

tional art in the synagogue and their opponents. The struggle has not yet ended, for we still find echoes of it reverberating down to our own times.[1]

The earliest surviving monuments of antiquity to contain Jewish symbols and cult objects derived from the Hebrew Bible and associated with the temple-worship are to be found in the coins of the Hasmonaean dynasty. The half and quarter shekels of bronze struck in 136/5 B.C., the fourth and last year of the reign of Simon Maccabaeus, depict on the obverse the *ethrōgh*, with stalk pointing upward between two bundles of twigs—designed no doubt to represent the *lūlābh* (Pl. I. 1).[2] In the small bronze coins of Antigonus Mattathias, the last of the Hasmonaean rulers (40–37 B.C.), we meet with a copy of the Mᵉnōrāh, the seven-branched candlestick, destined to become so favourite a type for reproduction (Pl. I. 2). Of the later coins, the tetradrachms of the Second Revolt (A.D. 132–5) contain on the obverse one object whose interpretation has presented difficulties.[3] According to the best numismatic opinion it represents the curtain (*pārōkheth*) in the Tabernacle before the Holy of Holies—shown by four fluted columns—with the Ark of Mercy within, the latter indicated by an arched structure with two horizontal cross-pieces (Pl. I. 3).[4] An-

---

[1] For typical examples of the Rabbinical attitude towards art, see the article by David Kaufmann, 'Art in the Synagogue', in *JQR* ix (1897), 254–69.

[2] The twigs of myrtle form part of the *lūlābh*, of which the other constituents are the shoot of a palm-tree and two willow-branches.

[3] G. F. Hill, *Catalogue of the Greek Coins of Palestine*, 1914, p. cv f.

[4] This view has the weighty support of Sir George Hill. See his *Catalogue of the Greek Coins of Palestine*, 1914, pp. cv–cvi. Attractive as this interpretation is, it would perhaps be an improvement to describe the object as the *pārōkheth* before the Holy of Holies in the *Temple* rather than in the Tabernacle. Since the Temple had replaced the Tabernacle as the sacred shrine of the Jews, there would not be so much point in reproducing an object like the latter, which had long ceased to exist, whereas the Temple was still fresh in the minds of the people. For the view, which has much to commend it, that the scene represents the Temple and that the central structure is the podium, see A. R. S.

other cult object found on the coins of the Second Revolt are the two silver trumpets—the *ḥăṣōṣᵉrōth* of the Hebrew Bible—so often used on festal occasions in Biblical and post-Biblical times. These are found on the reverse of the coins, with their mouthpieces pointing downwards (Pl. 1. 4).

We can obtain a clearer idea than is provided through the exiguous medium of coins as to how the cult objects looked, when we examine the bas-reliefs carved upon the celebrated arch of Titus (Pl. 1. 5). Upon it we find a representation of the golden Mᵉnōrāh and the Table of the Shewbread, both objects conveying an impression of massiveness. They are shown borne upon the shoulders of the victorious legionaries. Against the Table of the Shewbread recline the trumpets, which, like the Table itself, are here represented for the first time, although we find them again half a century later in the coins of the Second Revolt. The Mᵉnōrāh depicted on the Arch reveals one surprising feature. The pedestal is embossed with figures of dolphins. Such an innovation has, it need hardly be said, no Biblical sanction, nor would the Rabbis have countenanced this departure from tradition. But we must remember that we are dealing with Herod's Temple. When Herod gave his

Kennedy, *PEFQS*, 1914, p. 198 f. (quoted from S. A. Cook, *The Religion of Ancient Palestine*, 1930, pp. 195–6).

A different explanation has been put forward by J. C. Sloane, Jr., in *JQR* n.s. xxv. 6–12, where he argues that this object represents the Tōrāh shrine. See against this Helen Rosenau, in *PEFQS*, July 1936, 157–62. Sloane also claims that the frontispiece to the Ashburnham Pentateuch represents the Ark of the Law. Against this it may be said that a representation of so characteristic a piece of synagogue furniture as a Tōrāh shrine would fall outside the orbit of Christian art, whereas the Temple often figures in Christian miniatures to illustrate such themes as the Presentation, &c. An interesting form of syncretistic symbolism is provided by a Smyrna manuscript of Kosmas Indikopleustes, which Strzygowski reproduces in his *Bilderkreis des griechischen Physiologus*, p. 54 f. We are there shown a number of illustrations in which Jewish cult objects are associated with the Virgin Mary. The Mᵉnōrāh, the Tabernacle, Aaron's Staff, and the Table of the Shewbread are identified with various attributes of the Virgin.

orders to his (presumably) Hellenistic craftsmen for new copies of the cult vessels to be made, he was hardly likely to give much weight to any Rabbinical objections which might have been advanced.[1] More than any other of the cult objects the Menōrāh impressed itself upon the popular imagination. We are not, therefore, surprised to find it occupying for many centuries a place in the religious art of the Jews almost comparable to the Cross in Christian art.[2] We find reproductions of the Menōrāh everywhere, upon coins, medallions, the walls, mosaic floors, and door-heads of synagogues, in sculpture, gilded glass, and catacombs. Of some eighty-three decorated catacombs at Monte Verde seventy-eight show the Menōrāh.[3] This predilection for the Menōrāh was due to the deep symbolical significance with which it was invested by the Jewish imagination, over and above its strictly ritual character. It had come to be regarded as the symbol of immortality, the assurance of the continuity and indestructibility of the people and its faith. The Jewish mind, which was so often exercised by the eternal antinomies of light and darkness, fertility and sterility, good and evil, sin and atonement, found in the Menōrāh an object of peculiar fitness to express symbolically the undying spirit of Judaism.[4]

[1] Herod's Temple was considered profaned by Josephus because it was decorated with images of lions (*Vita*, 65. See E. R. Goodenough, *By Light, Light*, 1935, p. 258). The placing by Herod of a golden eagle upon the chief gate of his new Temple met with similar disapproval from Josephus (*Arch.* xvii, § 151. See E. Bevan, *Holy Images*, p. 48).

[2] An interesting example of adaptation, where the Cross takes the place of the Menōrāh, is cited by S. A. Cook, *The Religion of Ancient Palestine in the Light of Archaeology*, London, 1930, p. 226. It was found in the ruins of el-Ḥammām. The Menōrāh is rarely found in Christian illuminated manuscripts. The Smyrna copy of Kosmas Indikopleustes shows it (*supra*, p. 15, note). Of western manuscripts, there exists a privately owned Psalter, where the Menōrāh is introduced in a miniature depicting the Virgin Mary.

[3] Wischnitzer-Bernstein, *Gestalten und Symbole der jüdischen Kunst*, p. 67.

[4] For the symbolical significance of lamp and light in ancient Palestine, see S. A. Cook, op. cit., pp. 86–8.

ARCHAEOLOGICAL BACKGROUND

The specimens of Jewish gilded glass—most of them unfortunately fragmentary—found in the catacombs at Rome and elsewhere provide in a compact form a series of the most characteristic cult objects. Most of this gilded glass appears to belong to the fourth century, but a considerably earlier date has been claimed for one rather battered example, now in the Vatican, containing a Greek instead of the usual Latin inscriptions.[1]

This presumably early specimen, although markedly stylized, shows a freshness of execution wanting in its fellows. In contrast to the other examples, it possesses a landscape as a background, in this instance composed of huts and palm-trees. A row of columns surmounting three sides of the central picture, which de Rossi was the first to interpret as representing the columns of the Temple, succeeds this background.[2] The central picture shows a gabled building representing, according to de Rossi, the façade to the Holy of Holies in the Temple.[3] Below this structure appears the Mᵉnōrāh, flanked on either side by vessels used for ritual purposes, and the *lūlābh* and *ethrōgh* (Pl. II. 1). The later gilded glass discards both the landscape and the rows of columns. Moreover, the façade to the Holy of Holies in the Temple (if we accept that interpretation of it) yields place to a representation of the Ark of the Law, thus revealing the shift of emphasis from the sentimental attachment for the Temple to the living tradition of the Tōrāh.

A typical example of the later gilded glass is provided by a piece in the Kaiser Friedrich Museum in Berlin

---

[1] See Cohn-Wiener, *Die jüdische Kunst*, p. 128. A specimen of Jewish gilded glass at the British Museum is described in O. M. Dalton's *Guide to the Early Christian and Byzantine Antiquities*, 1921, p. 185 (Table Case B).

[2] See de Rossi's article, 'Verre représentant le temple de Jérusalem', in *Archives de l'Orient latin*, t. ii, pp. 493 f.

[3] Sukenik vigorously challenges the generally accepted interpretation of this picture. He claims that it represents a Tōrāh shrine. See his *Ancient Synagogue of Beth Alpha*, Jerusalem, 1932, pp. 20–1.

(Pl. II. 2). It is divided into two compartments. In the upper part, the Ark of the Law occupies the centre of the picture. It is shown open, with the ends of the scrolls of the law visible. It is flanked on either side by a Mᵉnōrāh. In between the spaces appear, from right to left, the palm-branch, citron, an amphora, and the ram's horn (*shōphār*). On the bottom of the lower compartment we can see a dish containing fish.[1] The depiction of this dish may be possibly taken to indicate the Sabbath symbolically.

Another specimen portrays the same cult objects, but is interesting for its manner of presentation of two of these objects (Pl. II. 3). The Ark of the Law is shown open, flanked on each side by a dove holding in its beak the end of a curtain-cord. The curtain itself, whose existence is thus implied, is not visible. Underneath the Shrine we have the Mᵉnōrāh, guarded on each side by a crouching lion. The presence of birds is particularly worth noting, as we shall find this motif helping us to explain some of the illuminations in the Christian Biblical manuscripts.

The discovery of gilded glass in the Jewish catacombs of Rome has presented a similar problem to scholars as its appearance in Christian catacombs. The usual explanation is that it is supposed to represent the 'Ḳiddūsh', or sanctification cups used on Sabbaths and Festivals prior to the beginning of meals. A theory put forward by Berliner is that it is to be interpreted as the 'cup of consolation' offered to mourners.

The Jewish catacombs contain symbols analogous to those found on the gilded glass. The Mᵉnōrāh, which at once establishes the Jewish character of the grave—it is sometimes difficult otherwise to distinguish Jewish from Christian graves—is the most frequently depicted, as I have mentioned before. In the catacomb at Rome by the Via Nomen-

---

[1] The custom amongst Jews of eating fish on the Sabbath Eve is of such antiquity that we find it already referred to in the satires of Persius (Satire 5, 176–88). See T. Reinach, *Textes d'Auteurs grecs et romains relatifs au Judaisme*, Paris, 1895, pp. 264–5.

tana, for example, a representation of the Ărōn haḵ-ḵōdhesh (the cabinet containing the scrolls of the law) is shown, flanked on either side by a Menōrāh (Pl. III). Other symbols are a kind of fruit from which an ear of wheat sprouts. This object has been tentatively equated with the lūlābh and ethrōgh. An oil-vessel, which appears sometimes, has been shrewdly explained by Samuel Krauss[1] as a symbolic expression of the sentence in Ecclesiastes, 'A good name is better than precious ointment; and the day of death than the days of one's birth'.[2] Over and above its ritual significance, the presence of the shōphār may be accounted for when it is remembered that according to Jewish legend the ram's horn will be blown on the day of resurrection in order to waken the dead.

Interesting in this connexion are the Christian catacombs, gilded glass, and sarcophagi, and the symbols they contain. The main types drawn from the Hebrew Bible are: Adam and Eve; Noah and the Ark; the Sacrifice of Isaac; Moses striking the rock; the Passage of the Israelites through the Red Sea; the Ascension of Elijah; the Deliverance of Jonah; the Three Youths in the fiery furnace; and Daniel in the lions' den. A glass-disk of the fourth century, found at Cologne and now in the British Museum[3] is particularly interesting, as it contains, in addition to other scriptural subjects, an illustration of the Vision of Ezekiel in the Valley of the Dry Bones, a subject which is occasionally found treated in the later sarcophagi, but not apparently upon the walls of the catacombs. This illustration shows, in part, remarkable affinities with one of the wall-paintings in the synagogue at Dura, of which I shall speak presently. The recurrence of the above cycle of scenes from the Old Testament was traced back by David Kaufmann to the ancient Jewish sᵉlīḥāh beginning with Mī sheʿānāh, which is said during the Ten Days of Penitence,

[1] See S. Krauss in JE s.v. 'Catacombs'.
[2] Ecclesiastes vii. 1.
[3] No. 628. See Dalton, Guide (1921), p. 141, for an illustration.

and whose phrasing closely resembles the litany *Ordo commendationis animae*. The latter, which, as Kaufmann makes clear, was patterned upon the Hebrew original, commemorates the names of those steadfast men from the Hebrew Bible who were miraculously saved in the hour of their greatest danger. It is these miracles which so regularly form the subject of early Christian funerary art.[1] The absence of a representation of Ezekiel's vision of the Dry Bones is somewhat strange, as we should have thought it a subject peculiarly appropriate for depiction upon the Christian catacombs. Whatever the reason, Ezekiel is rarely represented in ancient Christian art. The omission, in so far as it concerns the catacombs, strengthens the force of Kaufmann's happy explanation. For we find that prophet mentioned neither in the Latin litany nor in its Hebrew archetype.

Like the Christians, until Christianity became first a tolerated and afterwards the State religion, the Jews of the Empire were largely restricted in their art to the expression of their religious ideas by means of symbols. The difference of the religious approach between Jew and Christian is characteristically exemplified in the decorations which we find upon the catacombs and gilded glass. The Jew, we observe, emphasizes the teaching of the Tōrāh and the service of the synagogue. On the other hand, the Christian, as is to be expected, stresses the subject of redemption and salvation.

[1] See David Kaufmann, 'Sens et origine des symboles tumulaires de l'ancien-Testament dans l'art chrétien primitif,' in *RÉJ* xiv. 33–48; 217–53. Kaufmann dismisses, somewhat impatiently, the contention of Braun that the recurrence of certain types in early Christian art is derived from the Epistle to the Hebrews, ch. xi, where the writer enumerates notable instances from the Bible of those who had held fast to their faith in the hour of trial. Braun's happy suggestion does seem to explain satisfactorily the selection of some of the subjects in Christian iconography. Ecclesiasticus xliv–l, in praise of 'famous men', may provide a similar clue to the choice of subjects deemed suitable for pictorial treatment amongst the Jews. It is indeed remarkable how much of the iconographic matter of the Hebrew Bible is covered by these chapters from Ecclesiasticus and the *sᵉlīḥāh* beginning with *Mī sheʿānāh*.

So much for symbolic representations, an aspect of Jewish art which cannot be said to be artistically exciting, however valuable it may be historically. We enter upon a far more interesting phase of the subject when we turn to the historical art amongst the Jews. Up to a few years ago this aspect of the subject was almost a blank page in the history of Jewish art. Thanks to the recent excavations of ancient synagogues in Palestine, and above all, to the discovery—unique of its kind—of wall-paintings in the synagogue at Dura-Europos, a new and exciting chapter has been added to the history of Biblical art, whose deep significance and wide implications are being increasingly appreciated.

CHAPTER II
THE WALL-PAINTINGS AT DURA-EUROPOS

OF the general importance of Dura-Europos to archaeology, this is not the place to speak. Professor Rostovtzeff's recent book, *Dura-Europos and its Art*, gives a masterly résumé of the subject and sums up authoritatively its value and importance. Situated on the Middle Euphrates, some 250 miles east of the Syrian coast, and roughly in a line with Palmyra and Emesa, this Pompeii of the Syrian desert, as it has been happily called, produced no greater surprise to scholars than the remains, constituting about half of the original number, of a series of wall-paintings whose subjects, while mainly drawn from the Hebrew Bible, incorporated also elements from the later Hebrew literature and traditions. These paintings were found in a synagogue buried under a sloping embankment to the north of the main gate, and adjacent to the city wall, which ran immediately behind it.

It is thus to the embankment, which had been raised by the inhabitants of the city to stem the tide of the Sassanian invasion, that we owe the fortunate preservation of this unique series of frescoes.

The synagogue unearthed by Rostovtzeff and his collaborators under the auspices of the Yale Expedition and the French *Académie des Inscriptions et Belles-Lettres* was not the first to stand on the site. It had been rebuilt and enlarged to replace an earlier synagogue, which was originally a private house. To this earlier synagogue Rostovtzeff assigns a date of about A.D. 200. Its walls were painted, but the decorations were restricted to purely ornamental patterns. In the later synagogue, of which I propose to speak now, a building inscription in Aramaic declares that it was rebuilt by Samuel the archisynagogue in the year A.D. 245.

Rostovtzeff and his colleagues trace two stages, separated from each other by a short interval of time, in the history

THE WALL-PAINTINGS AT DURA-EUROPOS 23

of the decoration of the synagogue. In the first stage, only the niche in the west wall, which contained the Ark of the Law, and the panel above the niche, had paintings on them.[1] Upon the arcuated entablature of the niche we find a number of objects, with most of which we are already familiar from the Jewish catacombs and gilded glass (Pl. v. 1). In the centre we have a representation of what Rostovtzeff, following the interpretation of Sloane, describes as the Tōrāh shrine, but which may also be explained as the façade of the Holy of Holies in the Temple.[2] To the left of this picture we have the Meⁿōrāh and between it and the façade, the *lūlābh* and *ethrōgh*.[3] So far the objects present no surprises to us, but on the right of the representation of the façade we meet with something new in Jewish iconography —a painting of the Sacrifice of Isaac. The three human actors in the fresco are presented to us in a peculiar style. Instead of our seeing them frontally, a form so characteristic of Assyrian, Egyptian, and Iranian art, only the backs of the figures are shown, the heads being indicated by black spots. H. F. Pearson's acute suggestion to the effect 'that at first the management of the synagogue hesitated to allow human figures to appear in the decoration' seems to provide the solution to this peculiar style of painting.[4]

[1] M. Rostovtzeff, *Dura-Europos and its Art*, p. 106.
[2] Supra, pp. 14–15, note 4.
[3] In addition to being shown on coins and synagogue ornamentation, the *lūlābh* and *ethrōgh* have also been found on a Jewish seal (of the fourth century A.D.?) See S. A. Cook, op. cit., p. 194.
[4] Rostovtzeff, op. cit., p. 106. Such an attitude would be in conformity with the Rabbinic tradition, more particularly before the use of representational art in the synagogue was sanctioned. A remarkable example of this unwillingness to draw human faces is provided in later times by the Hebrew Bible B. 30 in the Ambrosian Library at Milan (cf. Pl. v. 2). Fol. 1 *b* contains, as a headpiece to Genesis, a representation of Adam and Eve. In both cases their faces are hidden by their locks. Similarly on fol. 182 *b*, the headpiece to Deuteronomy, Moses, who is depicted as receiving the Tables of the Law, has his face completely obscured by his hair. In the Hebrew *Maḥăzōr* at the Bodleian (no. 2373 in Neubauer) the face of God, who is drawn as a winged being,

The space above the arcuated entablature passed through two phases of painting. It resembles in consequence a particularly difficult palimpsest. The difficulty of separating the under-painting from the over-painting is enhanced by the flaking of the paint, and by the fading of the colours since the panel was first brought to light. The photographs so far published of this enigmatic panel are almost useless. Perhaps an ultra-violet ray photograph may help to elucidate its mysteries. In the absence of such help we must fall back upon the published accounts. Fortunately, the panel has been studied with great care by Professor Kraeling, to whom, and to Professor Pearson who collaborated with him, we are indebted for a most careful and conscientious description, as well as for an interesting if not always convincing interpretation.[1]

In the first phase, the panel, which was left undivided into registers or compartments, had painted upon it, on a red ground, a large tree, with luxuriant foliage, with two indistinct sacred utensils at its foot. So far I am following Professor Rostovtzeff's cautious description.[2] Professor Kraeling, who identifies the tree as a vine, shrewdly surmises that it has a symbolical significance. In this connexion the rather elaborate comparison of Israel with the vine found in Psalm lxxx. 4–17 might have been quoted with advantage.[3] When, however, Kraeling goes on to assert that the tree also symbolized national life and unity, he may perhaps be accused of reading too much into the picture. One other point may be mentioned. Concurrently with its identification of Israel, Jewish tradition appears to

is left blank. It will be recalled that illustrations of Muḥammad's Ascension in Islamic manuscripts show the face of the Prophet veiled.

[1] See *Rep.* vi. 367–71.   [2] *Dura-Europos and its Art*, p. 106.

[3] Cf. particularly vv. 14–15: 'Turn again, we beseech thee, O God of hosts: Look down from Heaven, and behold and visit this vine, and the stock which thy right hand hath planted, and the branch that thou madest strong for thyself.' The symbolism of the vine has also been taken over into Christian art and doctrine. See S. A. Cook, op. cit., p. 226, and M. R. James, *Apoc. N.T.*, pp. 36–7.

have associated the vine (amongst other trees) with the Tree of Life, whose symbolical representation may be traced back to remotest antiquity, while the history of its diffusion over so many countries and civilizations forms so fascinating a chapter of folk-lore.[1] In connexion with this fresco it is singularly appropriate that the oldest representations of what has been interpreted as the Tree of Life should come from the region of the Euphrates and the Tigris.[2] The cylinder seals recently discovered in Ur show a tree with a goat on each side.[3] Legrain assigns them to the first dynasty (*c.* 2850 B.C.). The choice of the vine receives additional significance when we recall the reference in Josephus to the golden vine in the Temple of Herod, with grapes as big as a man.[4] It also is pertinent to observe that the Tōrāh had come to be identified by this time with the Tree of Life. This conception is already implicit in the Book of Proverbs, where wisdom is praised as 'the tree of life to those who hold fast to her, and happy is every one who retains her' (iii. 18). As the Tōrāh was regarded as the source of all wisdom, it naturally came to be associated and identified with the Tree of Life. The Talmūdh and the liturgy carry this idea a stage farther. In the tractate *Taʿănīth* of the Babylonian Talmūdh we read:

[1] See Z. Ameisenowa, 'The Tree of Life in Jewish Iconography,' in the *Journal of the Warburg Institute*, ii. 326–45.

[2] So interpreted by Z. Ameisenowa, l.c., p. 329.

[3] The same motif, it may be recalled, occurs, in combination with other elements, in the famous Taanach terra-cotta incense altar or incense burner of *c.* 700–600 B.C. See S. A. Cook, op. cit., pp. 61–2. A Babylonian seal at the British Museum (no. 89326) depicts a tree standing 'between two figures, behind one of which is a serpent. It is now interpreted as a god with his worshipper partaking of the fruit of the 'tree of life'. See Cook, ib., p. 70.

[4] *Bell. Jud.* v. 210. See Z. Ameisenowa, l.c., p. 331, where the reference to Josephus in footnote 4 needs correcting. Dr. Ameisenowa apparently confuses Philo with Josephus, for it is the latter, not the former, who speaks of the giant vine, with grapes as big as a man. The *Apocalypse of Baruch* (xxix. 5) stresses the size and fertility of the vine as a characteristic of the Messianic age. See also *Pᵉsiḳtā Rabb.*, 75 *b*.

'Rabbi Naḥmān, the son of Isaac, said: Why are the words of the Tōrāh compared to a tree? Because of the verse in the Scriptures, It is a tree of life to those who take hold of her (Prov. iii. 18).'[1]

Another passage on the same page reinforces this analogy:

'Whosoever studies the Tōrāh for its own sake will draw from it the medicine of life, in accordance with the verse, It is a tree of life to them that take hold of her.'[2]

The service in the synagogue provides additional proof in support of the identification in the people's mind of the Tōrāh with the Tree of Life. As the scroll of the Law is replaced in the Ark, the cantor chants the above mentioned and the preceding verse from the Book of Proverbs. The same verses, it may be noted, together with others similarly eulogizing the Tōrāh, are often set out ornamentally round the title-pages of printed Hebrew Bibles and the borders of manuscript copies of the same work.

Other aspects of the Tree of Life may be pointed out. In the locus classicus in *Midhrash Kōnēn*, where the Gan ʿĒdhen, the Messianic Paradise, is described, we are given details which bring into clearer relief the choice of this symbolical representation. The description is so appropriate to our subject that I hope I may be forgiven for quoting it at some length.

'The third chamber of the Gan ʿĒdhen,' we are told, 'is built of silver and gold ornamented with pearls (these jewels symbolize the sun, moon, and stars respectively). It is very spacious, and contains the best of heaven and earth, with spices, fragrance, and sweet odours. In the centre of the chamber stands the Tree of Life, so high that it would take 500 years to reach its top. Under its shadow rest Abraham, Isaac, and Jacob, the tribes, those of the Egyptian exodus, and those who died in the wilderness, headed by Moses and Aaron. There are also David and Solomon, crowned,

---

[1] 7 a אמר רב נחמן בר יצחק למה נמשלו דברי תורה כעץ שנאמר עץ חיים היא למחזיקים בה. Naḥmān bar Isaac was a Babylonian Āmōrā of the fifth generation, who died in A.D. 356.

[2] Ibid. כל העוסק בתורה לשמה תורתו נעשית לו סם חיים שנאמר עץ חיים היא למחזיקים בה.

and Chileab attending upon his father David (2 Sam. iii. 3, *Shabbāth* 55 *b*). Every generation of Israel is represented except that of Absalom and his confederates. Moses teaches them the Law and Aaron gives them instruction. The Tree of Life is like a ladder upon which the souls of the righteous ascend and descend.¹

It is from these and similar accounts that we can appreciate the significance of the choice of the Tree of Life as a theme for representation, and the reason for the special place of honour it was assigned in the synagogue. The drawing of the tree upon so large a scale is easily understandable when we consider the size with which legend has invested its prototype. The central conception underlying the painting in its first phase emerges somewhat more clearly when we interpret it as a representation of the Messianic paradise, although some of the details still need clarifying.²

So far we have been dealing with the first stage in the history of the decoration of the synagogue, represented by the painting upon the arcuated entablature of the niche and by the picture of the tree upon the wall above it. The second stage of this history, which must have followed soon after the first—the whole life of the synagogue barely comprising more than approximately a decade—marks a far more ambitious and artistic plan on the part of the management. It was decided to embellish the whole area of the walls, up to a certain height, with paintings, beginning with the uppermost zone first and working downwards. Even the large panel containing the tree, about which I have just spoken, was brought into the new scheme of decoration and had paintings superimposed upon it. Of the four registers of different heights into which the walls were divided, the lowest, forming the dado, was cut up into oblong panels of different sizes. Some of them were stippled in imitation of coloured marble, alternating with paintings

---

¹ Midrash Kōnēn, in *Arzē Lᵉbhānōn*, 3*a–b*, Venice, 1601; cf. Jellinek, *Beth ha-Midrasch*, ii. 28, 29. See also Z. Ameisenowa, l.c., p. 336.

² Students of Christian symbolism will recall that the *tree*, more particularly the palm-tree, associates the landscape with Paradise.

of lions, leopards, tigers, and masks of human faces, enclosed in rectangular and circular frames. The dado is of little interest for our purpose, as it does not appear to reveal any distinctively Jewish influences and conforms stylistically to the decoration prevalent at the time in Dura. It is far otherwise with the three remaining registers, which, following the example of Kraeling and others, we will call A, B, and C respectively, beginning with the uppermost register first. These were all painted with frescoes illustrating subjects drawn from the Hebrew Bible and Midhrāsh. Each panel was divided from its neighbour by broad black bands through which wavy lines were introduced as ornaments. The registers were similarly separated. These unique wall-paintings form so important a link in the transmission of Hebrew and Christian iconography, and the problems which they raise are so far-reaching that it will be necessary to deal with them at some length. I ought to say that I have not, unfortunately, had the opportunity yet of seeing the actual frescoes either *in situ* or in their new home in the Museum at Damascus. Thanks, however, to the excellent photographs which have been published from time to time, a personal examination of the frescoes, while eminently desirable, particularly for the understanding of the obscure and badly preserved specimens, need not be considered an indispensable prerequisite for their study.

To begin first with the central section of the western wall, upon which the eyes of the congregation would be focused as they entered the synagogue. In the first stage of decoration, as it may be remembered, this contained a large tree, of whose interpretation I have already spoken, together with some other subjects less easy to identify or interpret. When the more ambitious scheme of decoration was taken in hand this large panel was divided into two registers in conformity with the general plan. The original picture was painted over with a red wash and new frescoes were superimposed upon the old surface. Unfortunately the new painting has flaked so badly that it is difficult to make them out.

One of the most interesting and significant paintings occurs in the lower register (B) of the central panel. It depicts a figure resembling the traditional representations of Orpheus playing upon the lyre (Pl. vi. 1). In front of him are two large beasts, who appear to be charmed by the music. To the right of the animals are to be seen two birds in between the branches of the great vine. Kraeling could not account satisfactorily for the presence of these beasts, because he did not connect them with the player upon the lyre.[1] He assumed, too, that the animals belonged to the first phase of the mural decoration, an assumption which added to his difficulties. For it is clear that if the lyre-player belonged to the second phase of the decoration, so did the animals, as the latter form an integral part of the picture. The question which we ask ourselves is how to account for the intrusion of a figure resembling Orpheus, upon the walls of a synagogue. The answer does not seem difficult. The picture is most probably intended to represent King David, whose love for music and proficiency in playing it, was, in popular esteem, no less great than that of Orpheus. The artists, whether they were Jewish or non-Jewish, adopted the current representation of Orpheus for their own purpose. We shall see the same thing done in the Ezekiel panel, where the traditional figures of Psyche and the Zephyrs are incorporated into the picture. Whether this debt to the Orpheus myth extended beyond the pictorial is a question which need not be discussed here. One other point emerges. Are we justified in treating this picture as a paradisal scene? Its proximity to the great vine would tend to support this suggestion. In this connexion it must be remembered that according to some authorities, notably Strzygowski, the promise of a future life is implicit in the Orpheus myth. Our painting bears a distinct resemblance to the well-known 'Orpheus mosaic' discovered at Jerusalem

[1] *Rep.* vi. 371, note 72.

in 1901 (Pl. vi. 2). The Phrygian cap which the player upon the lyre wears is characteristic both of the painting and the mosaic. Thus Jewish as well as Christian religious art are found to be indebted to the current representations of the Orpheus myth. Orpheus came to serve as a model both for Christ in the rôle of the Good Shepherd, and for the music-loving David.[1]

In the same register but beneath this adaptation of the Orpheus myth, it is now possible, thanks to the drawing published by Du Mesnil, to distinguish two other episodes described in the Hebrew Bible. They are, Jacob blessing his twelve sons (on the left), and, on the right, the same patriarch blessing the two sons of Joseph—Ephraim and Manasseh.[2] This latter theme, it need hardly be said, is one which we constantly meet with in both Christian and Jewish illuminated manuscripts, and which came to be so favourite a subject with artists in later times.

The upper compartment of this central panel (in Register A), which, like the lower, is very badly damaged, contains, according to Rostovtzeff, 'a king in Iranian dress seated on his throne and surrounded by two men in Greco-Syrian and several in Iranian dress'. 'The king', says Rostovtzeff, 'may be David.'[3] To Kraeling, on the other hand, the picture suggests Moses *ex cathedra*, surrounded by the major and minor prophets.[4] To account for the sixteenth figure in the

---

[1] See S. A. Cook, *Religion of Ancient Palestine*, p. 228, for a brief but authoritative account of the significance of the 'Orpheus mosaic', as well as for the reference to Strzygowski. For a recent account of the Orpheus myth in Christian art the reader should refer to the article by H. Leclercq, in the *Dictionnaire d'Archéologie chrétienne*, s.v. 'Orphée'.

[2] *Les Peintures de la Synagogue de Doura-Europos*, Roma, 1939, pl. xxiii. M. Aubert in the *Gazette des Beaux-Arts*, July–Aug., 1938, p. 5, asserts that a Byzantine ivory in the British Museum reproduces exactly these two scenes. M. Aubert does not specify which ivory this is. But if, as papears most probable, it is the one described by Dalton in his *Guide* (1921) on p. 169 and reproduced on pl. v in that work, it would be incorrect to describe it as an 'exact' reproduction of the Dura painting.

[3] Op. cit., p. 109. [4] *Rep.* vi. 369.

fresco (excluding Moses), Kraeling brings in the prophet Daniel. In the drawing given in du Mesnil's recent work only fourteen figures are discernible in all.[1] In the face of such conflicting testimony and interpretation, we would do well to accept at the present stage only the first part of Rostovtzeff's suggestion that the central figure is that of a king.

Although the solution of this last enigmatic and much obliterated fresco is far from easy, I am tempted to offer another explanation. Rostovtzeff's tentative suggestion that it represents David involves us in a difficulty if we accept the king in a Phrygian cap playing on a golden lyre, in the panel immediately below it, as a picture of that monarch. Two representations of King David in such close proximity would require a good deal of explaining. I would suggest that this picture in the upper zone showing 'a king in Iranian dress seated on his throne and surrounded by two men in Greco-Syrian and several in Iranian dress' depicts Pharaoh confronted by Moses and Aaron, and the elders of Israel.[2] This explanation would account for the differentiation of dress in two of the figures, if we take them to represent Moses and Aaron. Additional support is lent to this suggestion when we remember that the painting appears in the same register and on the same wall as the long frieze portraying the Exodus, from which it is only divided by a narrow panel having as its subject Moses and the Burning Bush. Such a theme would therefore be in its right milieu. The same scene, it may be added, occurs frequently both in Christian iconography and in the medieval illuminated copies of the *Haggādhāh*.

---

[1] *Les Peintures de la Synagogue de Doura-Europos*, Roma, 1939, pl. xx.

[2] An early miniature depicting this scene is to be found in a Syriac MS. of possibly the seventh century (if not earlier), containing, when it was complete, the P^eshīṭtā version of the whole Bible. See H. Omont, *Peintures de l'ancien Testament dans un manuscrit syriaque du viie ou viiie siècle*, Paris, 1909. The same theme appears in the old basilica of St. Peter's in Rome.

One ought to say something now of the four narrow panels which adjoin the two large panels at both ends, the whole six thus forming, as Rostovtzeff points out, two triptychs. The four 'portrait panels', as they have been called, from the fact that each one of them contains a single figure, provide, with one exception, difficulties of interpretation. The exception is the panel on the right in the upper Register A. Here we are shown a vigorously executed fresco of Moses and the Burning Bush (Pl. VII. 1). Moses is presented to us frontally. He is dark-featured and wears long white clothes. His right hand, with the palm open, is extended into the thorn-bush, from which tongues of flame shoot. On the ground in front of him are the shoes which he has removed. We may observe, by the way, that Moses is presented to us as beardless, a form which early Christian and Byzantine art favours.

The most impressive of the four panels shows a man garbed in a long white dress. He is seen standing and reading from a scroll of the Law, which he is holding in his hands (Pl. VII. 2). The picture conveys an impression of great dignity and spiritual exaltation. It is perhaps the most striking of all the frescoes in the synagogue. The top panel on the left side of the niche, corresponding to the panel of Moses and the Burning Bush, is unfortunately mutilated. Only the bottom half is preserved, revealing the lower portion of a man clothed in a white dress, similar to those seen in the other portrait panels. His shoes, too, have been removed, and are on the ground in front of him. The fourth panel, which is immediately below this, has as its subject an old man, with grey hair and beard. Above him are seen the sun, moon, and stars. Such, in brief, is a factual description of these three panels, which we may well call 'problem pictures'. The question arises, whom do they stand for? The answer is not easy. Rostovtzeff[1] accepts, on the whole, the view of Professor E. R. Goodenough, who sees in all the four panels an attempt to depict the four pivotal stages

[1] *Dura-Europos and its Art*, p. 108.

THE WALL-PAINTINGS AT DURA-EUROPOS

in the history of Moses. To quote Goodenough's own words:

> 'Four scenes might well represent the great significant aspects of Moses' mystic career: the scene at the Bush; the scene on Sinai; Moses as the giver of the Mystic Torah; and the assumption of Moses.'[1]

This interpretation has the merit of consistency and coherence. It seeks to dispose of the individual problems by a general and comprehensive explanation. (I ought to mention here parenthetically that I cannot follow Goodenough in his linking up of these frescoes with the philosophy of Philo. It is, I think, extremely doubtful whether Philo's doctrines influenced to any appreciable extent the Jewish communities of Syria in the third century, except in so far as they derived from Rabbinic sources.) While not going all the way with him, we may consider his identification of the figure reading the law with Moses as both acute and deserving of general assent.[2] Far less convincing are Goodenough's identifications with Moses of the two remaining portrait panels to the left of the niche and corresponding to the two on the right. Let us take the top panel first, of which there are now only left the trunk and nether limbs of a man dressed in a white robe (Pl. VIII. 1). In front of him are a pair of shoes. To say that this picture represents Moses on Mount Sinai presupposes that the artist has introduced a detail—I refer to the shoes—for which there is no Biblical or, as far as I know, Rabbinic sanction. Moreover, four pictures of Moses seem a trifle too much. How much more likely that this picture represents Joshua, the heir and successor to Moses

---

[1] *By Light, Light*, p. 242.
[2] Du Mesnil ingeniously champions the claims of Ezra for this panel. See *Les Peintures de la Synagogue de Doura-Europos*, pp. 92–4. It is, however, not Ezra but Moses who figures as the Lawgiver in both Christian and Jewish iconography. Du Mesnil (ibid., p. 93) also makes the astonishing statement that the scroll was 'sans doute de papyrus'. The *Sēpher Tōrāh* could only have been written on one material —parchment.

and to the guardianship of the Tōrāh, and the only other figure in the Hebrew Bible who appears in a similar incident involving the removal of his shoes. How appropriate to have a picture of Moses and the Burning Bush balanced by one representing Joshua and the Angel.[1] This interpretation, moreover, paves the way for a better understanding of the fourth and last portrait panel. To complete the symmetrical scheme, the panel immediately below the mutilated picture in Register A would fit admirably if we could interpret it as an additional depiction of Joshua. And when we examine the picture closely we find that the details in it harmonize with such an interpretation. The introduction of the sun, moon, and stars clearly refers to Joshua bidding the sun and moon stay their courses (Pl. VIII. 2).[2] We should thus have two panels of Moses balanced by a similar number for Joshua, all the four occupying that position of honour to which they are so eminently entitled. If, on the other hand, we accept Goodenough's interpretation of all the four panels as portraying different phases in the life of Moses, we find ourselves involved in difficulties. I have already spoken of the difficulty in accepting such an interpretation in the case of the mutilated panel in Register A. We encounter even greater difficulties if we accept Goodenough's explanation of the fourth panel as the assumption of Moses. We should be forced to invest the hero of this picture with semi-divine attributes. We find Rostovtzeff, for example, in following the lead given by Goodenough and elaborating his description, compelled to take up an inherently false position towards this picture. He says of it:

---

[1] The so-called Second Nuremberg *Haggādhāh* depicts on two successive pages (fols. 37*b*, 38*a*) miniatures of Moses unrolling a scroll of the Law and of Joshua and the Angel. See *Die Haggadah von Sarajevo*, p. 168.

[2] Sukenik very briefly suggests a similar explanation. See his *Ancient Synagogues of Palestine and Greece*, p. 84. It is interesting to note that these two incidents relating to Joshua appear next to each other in a miniature in the Paris Gregory (fol. 226 *b*).

THE WALL-PAINTINGS AT DURA-EUROPOS 35

'Moses is presented here somewhat in the character of one of the great founders of new religions of the ancient world, as a canonised and almost deified hero, founder of the Jewish religion; a counterpart in some degree of Buddha and Christ.'[1]

Now, to put forward such an explanation is seriously to misapprehend the spirit of Rabbinic Judaism. It is difficult to believe that the heads of the community would have tolerated the presence of a picture embodying such an heretical conception upon the walls of their synagogue. Judaism, like Islam, set its face against the deification or semi-deification of its heroes. To have done so would have been considered a derogation from the indivisible unity of God. The idea of presenting Moses as a semi-divine hero would have been as repugnant to the religious heads of those days as it would be now.[2]

The plan shown on Plate IV gives some idea of the distribution of the wall-paintings. The synagogue was oriented towards Jerusalem, that is to say, the wall from which the niche projected was turned in a south-westerly direction. As we can see from the plan, only about half of the total number of the frescoes have survived, some of them in a very fragmentary state. The south-west wall is the best preserved, the other walls having been cut down in order to build the sloping embankment. It is, with the exception of a small portion in Register A on the left of the central panels, intact. To the right of this central area we have a long frieze illustrating the Exodus from Egypt and the passage of the Israelites through the Red Sea (Pl. XII. 1). In the first compartment, beginning from the extreme right, we are shown a fortified city wall. The next compartment introduces us to four marching columns of Israelites, some clad in the garb of warriors and equipped

---

[1] Op. cit., p. 108.
[2] Goodenough (*By Light, Light*, p. 259) is scarcely justified in saying that Judaism would have repudiated the frescoes of the synagogue at Dura. What Judaism would have repudiated is the un-Rabbinic interpretation placed upon them by Goodenough.

with shields, spears, and helmets, others unarmed and dressed in short tunics and carrying various objects, these possibly representing the spoils obtained from the Egyptians. One column of twelve people is, as Kraeling observes, intended to represent the 'elders of the Twelve Tribes'.[1] Moses, who is drawn in heroic proportions, marches in front of this host, his rod held high above him. The remaining sections of this frieze show us respectively the drowning of Pharaoh and his army in the Red Sea, and the Israelites marching on dry land, with Moses and Aaron bringing up the rear.

Unfortunately, the paintings to the left of the central panels are too damaged to identify with any measure of certainty or probability. Kraeling suggests the theme of Solomon and the Queen of Sheba for the one nearest the central area.

This disposes of Register A in the south-west wall. Registers B and C in this wall are happily intact and are, with the exception of the two portrait panels, reasonably free from difficulties. Starting, as we did in Register A, with the right section of the wall, we are confronted with two panels. The significance of the first on the right is clear. It shows the entrance to the Temple of Dagon. The ground in front is strewn with broken idols. To the left of this is seen the Ark of the Covenant, resting on a cart drawn by two cows. The fresco follows the Biblical account so closely that comment or elucidation are scarcely necessary.

The next scene introduces us to a representation of a Corinthian temple (Pl. ix. 1). The presence of a (presumably) pagan temple in a synagogue seems in the eyes of some scholars to strike an incongruous note, and has caused them a good deal of bewilderment.[2] Comte du Mesnil du Buisson offers two suggestions. One is that it represents Solomon's

---

[1] *Rep.* vi. 345.

[2] Rostovtzeff, for example, calls this 'an enigmatic picture, which has not been satisfactorily explained' (*Dura-Europos and its Art*, p. 110).

Temple, the other, that it is a picture of the Temple of the Sun at Beth-Shemesh.[1] The latter explanation can scarcely be seriously considered. One can see no valid reason for the introduction of such a theme as the pagan temple at Beth-Shemesh, more particularly as the Hebrew Bible makes no reference to its existence. A study of the illuminated *Haggādhōth* of the Middle Ages may help us to explain this picture. We are often shown there a representation of a building which, we are told, is the restored Temple (Pl. IX. 2).[2]

Since the destruction of their State in A.D. 70 the Jews have tenaciously clung to the hope of having their Temple restored to them once again. The Jewish liturgy is full of references to such a restoration. This picture and the one representing the High Priest officiating may thus have been intended not only to recall to the Jews the splendour of their past, but also to embody their pious aspirations for the restoration of their Temple and its service. That the artist should here paint a copy of a temple in the prevailing architectural style should not cause us surprise. We could scarcely have expected him to paint the picture with historical fidelity.

To the left of the central panel and in the same register we have a representation of a High Priest in a sacrificial setting (Pl. x). Professor Kraeling, whose admirably lucid

[1] *Rep.* vi. 348.
[2] Reproduced from *Die Haggadah von Sarajevo*, facsimile 32. The inscription there reads: בית המקדש שיבנה במהרה בימינו ('The Temple, may it be speedily rebuilt in our days.') In his recent book (*Les Peintures de la Synagogue de Doura-Europos*, Roma, 1939) du Mesnil puts forward a similar explanation to the above, qualifying it with a mark of interrogation. His alternative suggestion that the picture represents the Temple of the Sun at Beth-Shemesh still stands, the author leaving it to the reader to make his choice of one or other of these interpretations. ('Entre les deux explications proposées le lecteur choisira celle qui lui paraîtra la plus vraisemblable.') Du Mesnil is apparently unaware of illustrations of the restored Temple appearing in copies of the *Haggādhāh*.

account I have here and elsewhere laid under tribute, calls it 'The Aaronic Priesthood'.[1] By adopting this title Kraeling seems to be needlessly creating difficulties for himself. The background of the picture is not, as we should expect if we followed Kraeling, of the Tabernacle in the wilderness, but of some far more elaborate structure—in fact, a temple. Kraeling appears to have been misled by the name of Aaron written in Greek over the picture. It is possible, however, that it was not the artist who was responsible for this caption, but some visitor, who may have done it after the synagogue had fallen into neglect. But granted even that the artist was responsible, we should still treat the painting critically rather than accept unquestioningly the description provided by him.

The fresco shows a Corinthian temple surrounded by a wall into which three gates have been pierced. The Ark of the Covenant is seen before a draped curtain. In front of it is the Mᵉnōrāh, with small incense-burners to the right and left. On the right is an altar, on which is laid a white sacrificial animal. In the temple-court stands the High Priest in his ceremonial robes. The name Αρων is painted above the figure. To the right and left priestly servants are standing, with sacrificial animals by them. Kraeling tries hard to reconcile this picture with the account given in the Pentateuch. The difficulties seem to me to vanish, if we realize that what the artist intended to represent was a generalized picture of a High Priest officiating in the Temple, rather than a representation of Aaron in the Tabernacle. Both Kraeling and Rostovtzeff have been too ready to assume that the panel represented Aaron, on the strength of an inscription for which we have no warrant to say that it was made by the artist.[2] How deeply the ceremonial of the High Priest had impressed itself upon the people may be gathered, for example, from the glowing description of Aaron in Ecclesiasticus, ch. xlv, and the more

---

[1] Rostovtzeff follows Kraeling in calling this picture 'The High Priest Aaron' (op. cit., p. 110).   [2] Rostovtzeff, op. cit., p. 110.

THE WALL-PAINTINGS AT DURA-EUROPOS 39

elaborate account in the same Book of the High Priest Simon in ch. l.

The last picture in this register appearing on the same wall, has been made the subject of some very acute comment by Kraeling. He describes it as 'Miriam's Well', to which identification he appends a question mark (Pl. XI. 1).[1] Against the background of the Tabernacle are seen to the right and left twelve tents, six on each side. In front of each of the tents, a man is shown holding in his raised hand a staff. Twelve streams empty from the tents into a large well in the centre. By its side stands Moses, drawn on an heroic scale, and shown striking the well with his staff. As Kraeling observes, the picture appears to embody elements from different sources, drawing both upon Bible and Midhrāsh.[2] He rightly draws our attention to the Aggadhic legend of Miriam's Well found, for example, in the Tōsephtā to the 'tractate Sukkah (3, 11–16) where it speaks of a miraculous well revealed to Miriam in order to still the murmurings of the Israelites at the lack of water. The well followed the Israelites during the whole of their wanderings in the wilderness. It took up its position in the midst of the camp, before the tabernacle, whenever the Israelites pitched their tents. Moses and the "elders" would thereupon appear before their tents and sing the Song of the Well (Num. xxi). Then the well would gush forth streams of water, which divided the camp into twelve parts.'[3]

Kraeling's interpretation of the panel is thus very helpful. He realizes, too, its connexion with the twelve wells of Elim. It is interesting to see how the illustrated *Haggādhōth* describe a similar scene. The celebrated *Haggādhāh* of Sarajevo has a miniature which represents according to the subjoined legend 'The Twelve Wells of Elim and the Seventy Palm-Trees' (Pl. XI. 2).[4] Another manuscript, the

[1] *Rep.* vi. 353–4.   [2] Ibid.
[3] Op. cit., p. 354. See also Ginzberg's *Legends of the Jews*, iii. 50–3; vi. 21, note 129. (This quotation is taken from Kraeling.)
[4] *Die Haggadah von Sarajevo*, facsimile 29; also p. 154. The description

so-called Second *Haggādhāh* of Nuremberg, illustrates a similar theme. Here a square four-cornered well does duty for the twelve fountains.[1] The depicting of the elders in our fresco with staves in their hands seems to recall the Song of the Well,

> 'The well which the princes digged,
> which the nobles of the people delved,
> with the sceptre, and with their staves.'[2]

As the captions to illustrations of this theme found in copies of illuminated *Haggādhōth* expressly refer to the oasis of Elim, we are, I think, justified in describing the present fresco by some similar title rather than, following Kraeling, as 'Miriam's Well (?)', although the shift of emphasis thereby involved is actually slight. The form of the story in which it is presented to us by the artist is, as Kraeling shrewdly remarks, 'a conflation of several accounts of the miraculous discovery of water in the desert'.[3]

We now arrive at Register C, the last of the registers and the best preserved. It owes this good fortune to the happy chance of the lower parts of the wall escaping demolition, when the synagogue was converted into a sloping embankment. The niche in the south-west wall divides this register into two parts, each of which contains two panels. The frieze on the extreme right introduces a reads: ויבאו אלימה ושם שתי עשרה עינות מים ושבעים תמרים. 'And they came to Elim, where were twelve springs of water and three score and ten palm trees' (Exod. xv. 27 [R.V.]). The wells and palms of Elim are mentioned in the Mt. Athos manual of painting. See M. R. James, *A Book of Old Testament Illustrations*, p. 14.

[1] Op. cit., p. 154.   [2] Numbers xxi. 18.
[3] *Rep.* vi. 354. One clue, hitherto overlooked, to the importance which the wells of Elim assumed in post-Biblical literature may be found in the writings of Philo. In *De Vita Mosis*, i. 188–90, Philo makes Elim the subject of an allegorical interpretation, which strikingly illuminates the form of the fresco at Dura. In explaining the reason for '*twelve* springs', he says: 'For the nation has twelve tribes, each of which, in virtue of its piety, will be represented by the well which supplies piety in perennial streams and noble actions unceasingly. . . .' (I quote from H. F. Colson's translation in the *Loeb Classics*, vol. vi, pp. 373–4).

theme made familiar to us by innumerable paintings. It depicts the rescue of the infant Moses from the waters of the Nile (Pl. xii).[1] Pharaoh is shown on the right seated on a throne by the banks of the river. He is attended by two courtiers, one of whom is seen writing down his orders. The two Jewish midwives Shiphrah and Puah are observed to the left. A woman, her bosom seemingly bared as a sign of mourning, bends down to the edge of the river. Although the fresco is badly preserved at this point there can be little doubt that the woman is intended to be shown consigning a male child to the Nile. She is probably the mother of Moses, thus providing the link of continuity with the rest of the frieze. The next section shows the discovery of the infant Moses in the bulrushes by the daughter of Pharaoh. Her three maids stand by the water's edge, waiting for her, their hands filled with various articles of the toilet. To the left of the princess two women are seen, the one handing the child over to the other. They are presumably Jochebed and Miriam, the mother and sister of Moses.[2]

The next picture in the same register portrays the anointing of David by Samuel. With David are his six brothers. Samuel, who is drawn on a somewhat larger scale than the rest, holds the horn filled with oil over the head of David.

It has been ingeniously suggested by du Mesnil[3] that the fresco owes its position over the archisynagogue Samuel's seat of honour as a well-designed compliment to him for bearing the same name as the prophet who anointed David. Like so many of the others in the synagogue, the fresco preserves for us the earliest extant form in which a scene from the Hebrew Bible is represented. Its interest is

---

[1] Kraeling's description to which I am greatly indebted misses the significance of some of the details. His account may be usefully supplemented by that of du Mesnil. For the former, see *Rep.* vi. 359; for the latter, *Revue biblique*, xliii. 550.

[2] Exodus i–ii.

[3] *Revue biblique*, xliii, p. 558. The suggestion receives from Kraeling only a qualified acceptance. See *Rep.* vi. 376.

further enhanced by the discovery of affinities in it with the celebrated Byzantine MS. at Paris (no. 510), containing the homilies of Gregory Nazianzenus.[1] A valuable link in the chain of transmission in O.T. illustration is thus established. As we shall see later, when we come to discuss the Ezekiel frieze, the same MS. provides an additional basis of comparison with a Durene fresco.

Of the two panels to the left of the niche, the first beginning from the right is one of the most animated and skilfully executed paintings of the whole series. The story of Esther as it is unfolded here is agreeably free from the fault of overcrowding, which disfigures so many of the other paintings (Pl. XIII).[2] There is some doubt as to whether the painting should be read from right to left or vice versa. Du Mesnil supports the former view, against Kraeling, who ably challenges the assumptions involved by such an interpretation. Following Kraeling and beginning from the left, we see Mordecai clad in regal garments and mounted upon a handsome white horse. It is led by Haman, who is shown wearing the ignominious garb of a menial. To the left of Haman are seen four figures in Graeco-Syrian dress, whom Kraeling explains as the bystanders witnessing the triumph of Mordecai. On the other hand, Rostovtzeff connects them with the succeeding section of the fresco.[3] This shows us King Ahasuerus seated upon a throne, with Queen Esther on his right. Behind her stands a female attendant. The king, who is apparently handing a message to his courier, is attended by a courtier and secretary, the latter depicted

---

[1] See H. Buchthal, *The Miniatures of the Paris Psalter*, London, 1938, pp. 18–21. I was myself struck with certain affinities between the Durene fresco and the miniature in the Paris Gregory before consulting this book. Buchthal adduces further parallels from other illuminated manuscripts, including, of course, the Paris Psalter, upon the basis of which he essays a reconstruction of the prototype. The date of the Paris Gregory is assigned on internal grounds to somewhere between 880 and 886. It was probably produced in Constantinople, 'in the immediate vicinity of the Imperial Court' (op. cit., p. 56).

[2] *Rep.* vi. 361.   [3] *Dura-Europos and its Art*, p. 112.

in the act of taking down the king's commands on his tablets. As an excellent view of the fresco could be commanded from the women's benches, it has been suggested that it was expressly placed there for that reason. This explanation receives additional support from a statement in the Babylonian Talmūdh to the effect that it was made compulsory by Joshua ben Levi for the women to attend the synagogue on the festival of Purim, in order to listen to the reading of the Book of Esther.[1]

The concluding panel in this register extending across the south-west wall has for its subject one of the most popular figures in Jewish history and legend, the prophet Elijah. No less than four, possibly five, of the extant frescoes, are devoted to conspicuous events in his career. The panel to the left of the Esther and Mordecai frieze depicts the prophet reviving the widow's son at Zarephath. The painting provides additional interest as a specimen of the art of continuous narration, which several of the other paintings also illustrate. On the left of the picture is shown the widow, dressed in dark clothes and her bosom bared in token of bereavement, holding in her arms her dead child. Elijah, to whom the widow is seen handing over her child, reclines on a couch, his arms encircling the boy. Above the head of the child and to the right of him the hand of God appears. The last section of the painting shows us the mother, dressed in less sombre clothes, joyfully clasping her living child in her arms.[2] The artist, it may be noted, has here

---

[1] Joshua ben Levi was a Palestinian Āmōrā, who flourished in the first half of the third century and was therefore contemporary with the frescoes. The reference is to be found in M*ghillāh* (T.B.) 4a.

[2] 1 Kings xvii. See *Rep.* vi. 362–3. As du Mesnil points out the picture could equally well be applied to Elisha and the Shunamite woman (2 Kings iv; see *Rev. bibl.* xliii. 117). But as the other frescoes deal with Elijah, and the graffiti also specially associate him with this painting, there is presumptive evidence in favour of this attribution. On the other hand, it is the story of Elisha and the Shunamite that forms the *Haphṭārāh* (the lesson from the Prophets) to the pericope *Vay-Yērā* (Gen. xviii–xxii).

succeeded in conveying the atmosphere of suspense and emotional tension very effectively (Pl. XIII).

Of the three remaining panels on the south-east wall in Register C, two are unmistakably connected with the prophet Elijah. The third is more doubtful, owing to its bad preservation. Kraeling interprets it as a representation of Elijah and the Widow's Cruse. The other two panels to the left of it illustrate two familiar episodes in the life of the prophet. The first starting from the left of the mutilated fresco depicts the theme of the false prophets sacrificing to Baal.[1] Standing round an altar upon which a bullock is laid are eight priests of Baal arrayed in long robes. One detail betrays the incursion of the Midhrāsh into the painting. Underneath the altar is seen a crouching figure preparing to light the fire, for which the prophets of Baal had so fruitlessly invoked their master. A large serpent spread in coils upon the ground frustrates the deceit of Hiel (for so he is called in the Midhrāsh) by slaying him.[2]

The third and last of these panels continues the story as told in the Book of Kings.[3] An altar, with a trussed bullock placed upon it, made ready for the sacrifice, occupies the centre of the picture. To the left are to be observed three figures, dressed in long white garments, each shown with a hand raised to heaven in supplication. One of these figures is obviously Elijah. The other two are probably priests. On the other side of the altar is a smaller figure also dressed in white robes. He, too, may be a (young) priest. Kraeling is, I think, wrong in suggesting that this person might be Elijah's servant. If he were that, he would be dressed in the garments of a servant. It is the other figure to the right of the altar who is actually dressed in such clothes, who is likely to be Elijah's lad.[4]

Before discussing the Ezekiel panel, which I have re-

---

[1] See *Rep.* vi. 363–4.

[2] *Yalḳūṭ Shimʿōnī*. See Ginzberg, *Legends of the Jews*, iv. 198 and vi. 319, note 15.

[3] 1 Kings xvii. 8–16.   [4] *Rep.* vi. 363.

served for the end, there remain a number of frescoes in various states of fragmentation, whose significance and interpretation are still an open question. Kraeling, who has studied them carefully and conscientiously, proposes the following solutions for them: Solomon and the Queen of Sheba, and Jacob's Dream, in Register A; The Ark brought to Mount Zion, and its capture by the Philistines, in Register B; and, lastly, David surprising Saul asleep, and Elijah fed by the ravens, in Register C. The happiest of these identifications is that of David surprising Saul. Perhaps the much mutilated fresco, which Hopkins connects with Noah, and Kraeling with Elijah being fed by the ravens, may really portray Abraham frightening the birds from the sacrifice, as the birds in question scarcely resemble ravens.

I have left to the last the fresco which has given the most trouble and has led to a number of interpretations each one more ingenious than the other. I refer to the long Ezekiel panel which stretches across the whole of Register C on the north-west wall (Pl. XIV). The first section of the painting, starting from the left, offers no great difficulties. It is at cnce apparent that it has reference to the prophet Ezekiel and to the Vision of the Dry Bones, as recounted in the thirty-seventh chapter of that book. The figure of the prophet attired in a tunic and trousers is twice repeated. He appears in each case with the hand of God stretching out from the sky in his direction. In the very first representation of the prophet, the hand of God grasps Ezekiel by the hair of his head, a detail which is not to be found in the thirty-seventh chapter, but in chap. 8, verse 3.

'And he put forth the form of an hand, and took me by a lock of mine head; and the spirit lifted me up between the earth and the heaven and brought me in the visions of God to Jerusalem.'

The fusion of elements in this fresco deriving from different portions of the book is particularly interesting, as it will help us to elucidate the more difficult parts of the frieze. The three representations of the prophet at intervals are possibly to be explained as a somewhat naïve attempt on the part of the artist at continuous narration, to present, one might almost say, the story in the form of a film.[1] The ground round about is strewn with limbs and decapitated heads of human beings. To the right the scene changes from a plain to hilly country. A large fissure divides the landscape into two mountain ridges, on each of whose summits stands a solitary tree. The same landscape, it may be noted, is to be found in a miniature depicting the same theme in the Paris Gregory (Pl. xv. 2).[2]

The wide fissure and a toppling building would seem to indicate that the artist intended to represent the scene of an earthquake, a point hitherto overlooked. At the foot of the hills are to be seen more mutilated limbs and decapitated heads, and, on the right, three corpses, symmetrically arranged in horizontal lines, one laid on the top of the other. It is difficult to reconcile this background of quaking hills and crumbling buildings with the thirty-seventh chapter of Ezekiel. No hint is given there of such a cataclysm. The next chapter, however, the thirty-eighth, supplies the very details we need in elucidation of the scene.

---

[1] The repetition of the figure of the prophet may perhaps be designed to illustrate the phrase—'And he caused me to pass by them round about' (xxxvii. 3).

[2] See W. Neuss, *Das Buch Ezechiel in der Kunst*, Münster, 1912, fig. 25 (facing p. 186), for a reproduction of this miniature. For a reproduction of the same in colours, see *Dictionnaire d'Archéologie chrétienne*, s.v. 'Ezechiel', coll. 1051–2. A comparison between the Durene fresco and the miniature in the Paris Gregory has been made by Gitta Wodtke in an article entitled 'Malereien der Synagoge in Dura und ihre Parallelen in der christlichen Kunst', in the *Zeitschrift für die neutestamentliche Wissenschaft*, Band 34, 1935, pp. 51–62. I was glad to see my own impression of the kinship between the two illustrations confirmed by the author of this article. In addition to a portion of the Ezekiel frieze the author deals also with two other frescoes. These are, the Discovery of the Infant Moses, and the very obscure subject which du Mesnil at one time identified with the Tribulation of Job, an attribution which Gitta Wodtke accepts without question. I am indebted to Dr. Hugo Buchthal for drawing my attention to this article.

The chapter, it may be remembered, describes the upheaval in the land of Israel at the approach of Gog. When we read that 'the mountains shall be thrown down, and the steep places shall fall, and every wall shall fall to the ground',[1] we are given the appropriate setting to the fresco. Moreover, Jewish apocalyptic literature provides further corroborative evidence. According to the Book of Baruch the prelude to the Day of Judgement was to include earthquakes, in addition to the plagues of the sword, famine and fire.[2]

The next section of the picture continues the Vision of the Valley of the Dry Bones. Over the head of Ezekiel are seen four fluttering winged creatures representing the four winds mentioned in verse 9 of the chapter. On the ground to the right a graceful figure bends over the inanimate bodies into which she breathes new life. The fresco thus here follows closely the description as given in Ezekiel:

'Then said he unto me, Prophesy unto the wind, son of man, and say to the wind, Thus saith the Lord God: Come from the four winds, O breath, and breathe upon these slain.'

The figures introduced into the picture, which bear such a striking resemblance to Psyche and the zephyrs, are, it is hardly necessary to say, borrowed from the current pagan art in Syria.

We now pass on to a new section of the panel, where our difficulties begin to increase. Flanked on either side by a figure in white linen garments, we see a group of somewhat smaller figures. They are also clad in long white robes, with their hands raised in praise and thanksgiving. The significance of this group seems clear enough. They are the 'exceeding great army' of the dead come to life again.[3] But whom do the two figures of impressive dignity repre-

---

[1] xxxviii. 20, in the Revised Version. Kraeling overlooks this reference, but cites other passages from Ezekiel. See *Rep.* vi. 357.

[2] See, for example, the Syriac *Apocalypse of Baruch* xxviii. 2–3. Cf. also Revelation viii. 5.

[3] Ezekiel xxxvii. 10.

sent? Kraeling inclines to the view that the figure on the left is that of the prophet, and, on the right, that of the leader of Israel restored. This view cannot, I think, be easily substantiated. There seems no valid reason, why the clothes of Ezekiel should have been changed from his customary tunic and trousers to white linen garments.[1] These two figures both clothed in white linen are certainly very mysterious. Do they represent one or two individuals? Ezekiel refers to a man clothed in linen in the ninth chapter of his book. It was he who was commanded to set a mark upon the foreheads of those who were to be spared from the general slaughter in Jerusalem. Rabbinic tradition identifies this person with the archangel Gabriel.[1] Jewish tradition assigns to him, together with the archangel Michael, an important part on the Day of Judgement. The last section of the panel lends some support to the interpretation here suggested that the two figures respectively portray Gabriel and Michael. Alternatively, they may both represent the archangel Gabriel.[2]

It is this last portion of the panel which has caused the greatest perplexity. Its obscurity leads Rostovtzeff, for example, to regret that 'the great scene of Ezekiel is so confused and difficult to interpret'.[3] Kraeling similarly struggles heroically but ineffectively to explain this mysterious episode.[4] Solutions have been offered in bewildering profusion. Hopkins sees in it the story of the violation of the right of sanctuary which Solomon committed when he had Joab executed in the sacred confines of the Tabernacle. Sukenik wishes to associate not only this section but the

---

[1] See, e.g., the commentary of Ḳimḥi upon Ezekiel ix. Daniel x. 4 also refers to this mysterious 'man clothed in linen'. Here, too, he is identified in Rabbinic exegesis with Gabriel.

[2] In the Paris Gregory, the figure of the archangel leading the prophet, in the miniature of the Vision of Ezekiel (fol. 438 b), may be either Michael or (less probably?) Gabriel (see Pl. xv. 2). An earlier miniature in that manuscript (fol. C b) depicts the Emperor Basil the Macedonian between the prophet Elijah and the archangel Gabriel.

[3] *Dura-Europos and its Art*, p. 124.   [4] *Rep.* vi. 355–9.

THE WALL-PAINTINGS AT DURA-EUROPOS 49

whole of the panel with the prophecies of Zachariah. Du Mesnil suggests the death of Ezekiel. Kraeling is inclined to interpret the figure on the altar as that of Zedekiah witnessing the executing of his son at Riblah. Finally, Aubert, more cautious than the rest, discreetly describes this section as 'Scène du Martyre'.[1] All this time the real solution lay close at hand. There was no necessity to go outside the Book of Ezekiel for the answer. Verses 1–6 of the ninth chapter supply the key to the painting. I may perhaps be permitted to quote them:

'Then he cried in mine ears with a loud voice, saying, Cause ye them that have charge over the city to draw near, every man with his destroying weapon in his hand. And behold, six men came from the way of the upper gate, which lieth toward the north, every man with his slaughter weapon in his hand; and one man in the midst of them clothed in linen, with a writer's inkhorn by his side. And they went in, and stood beside the brasen altar. And the glory of the God of Israel was gone up from the cherub, whereupon it was, to the threshold of the house: and he called to the man clothed in linen, which had the writer's inkhorn by his side. And the Lord said unto him, Go through the midst of the city, through the midst of Jerusalem, and set a mark upon the foreheads of the men that sigh and cry for all the abominations that be done in the midst thereof. And to the others [i.e. to the armed men] he said in mine hearing, Go ye through the city after him, and smite: let not your eye spare, neither have ye pity; slay utterly the old man, the young man and the maiden, and little children and women: but come not near any man upon whom is the mark; and begin at my sanctuary.' (R.V.)

These verses provide the appropriate setting to the picture. The brazen altar, the armed men commanded to slay, the man in linen garments, all fit in exactly with the painting. Additional confirmation of the correctness of this solution may be found in the illuminated Bibles. The famous twelfth-century Latin Bible, one of the treasures of the Lambeth Palace Library, has a miniature illustrating the very same theme.[2] On the page preceding the Book of

[1] *Gazette des Beaux-Arts*, tome xx, p. 23, fig. 15.
[2] Described by M. R. James, *A Descriptive Catalogue of the Manuscripts in . . . Lambeth Palace*, pt. 1, no. 3, pp. 2–9.

Ezekiel we are shown, in the lower compartment, the man in a linen garment, his ink-horn being indicated by a wallet at his girdle. To the right a group of five men draw their swords. The man in white makes the mark of the Tau on the foreheads of three men. To the right of this we see five executioners slay five or six men (Pl. XVI. 1). But perhaps a miniature in the late ninth-century MS. at Paris (Gr. 510), containing the homilies of Gregory Nazianzenus, reproduced by Neuss,[1] shows the clearest affinity with this section of the Ezekiel frieze (Pl. XV. 2). The Castilian Bible executed for Don Luis de Guzman in the early part of the fifteenth century, has a miniature which also shows striking similarities with the Dura fresco. Reading the miniature from left to right, we first of all see the man clothed in linen, here drawn as an angel, thus following the Jewish tradition which identifies him with Gabriel. In the centre is a representation of the Deity. To the left we have a group of six warriors (only the helmets are visible in the case of three of them), one of whom is slaying a man. To the right of these several figures are seen standing, their foreheads marked with the letter Tau (Pl. XVI. 2). The way these warriors are grouped in the manuscript is very like their arrangement in the Dura fresco, although an interval of twelve centuries separates the two illustrations. One of the most remarkable things to be observed in the history of iconography is the way in which the same details, setting, and treatment of a theme persist through the ages. Another example of parallel pictorial treatment can be observed if we compare the Ezekiel panel at Dura with a glass disk of Christian origin found at Cologne and now in the British Museum[2] (Pl. XV. 1; cf. Pl. XIV). A distinct likeness is to be noted between both these representations in the distribution and appearance of the mutilated limbs strewn around Ezekiel. The disk has been assigned to the fourth century and is thus later than the frescoes in the synagogue

---

[1] *Das Buch Ezechiel in der Kunst*, Münster (in Westf.), 1912, Fig. 25 (facing p. 186).   [2] See *Guide* (1921), p. 141, fig. 9.

of Dura. This raises the question of the extent of Jewish influence upon early Christian art, a subject which will be briefly discussed in the concluding chapter. Here it is sufficient to say that while it would be premature to dogmatize until the available material has been systematically studied, there can be no doubt that the frescoes at Dura will be found to have fundamentally altered our ideas upon this all-important question.

We can only deal in the very briefest manner with some of the other questions and problems which these frescoes raise. First, as to the arrangement. Can we discover any unifying thread in them, either in respect of their choice or sequence? One scholar, bolder than the rest, has ingeniously suggested that the three registers illustrate respectively the three aspects of the Jewish religion, the Law, the Covenant, and the Prophecies.[1] Unfortunately this suggestion, so characteristic of the neat precision of the Gallic mind, breaks down when seriously applied, the proposed divisions being far from satisfactory and made to stretch upon too rigid a bed of Procrustes. Our search for the underlying motive behind these frescoes might have been made easier, had the whole series been preserved. It is difficult to discover any single thread to bind them into an organic unity. A hitherto unexplored angle of approach is to study these frescoes in relation to the liturgy. Working on these lines we find that a number of the frescoes illustrate *Pārāshiyyōth* (pericopes) and certain *Haphṭārōth* read on Sabbaths and festivals. For example the story of the Exodus is read on Passover; the Vision of the Dry Bones in Ezekiel is the *Haphṭārāh* for the Sabbath falling during the same festival; Ezekiel xxxviii. 18–xxxix. 17 (against Gog, see supra, pp. 46–7) is read as *Haphṭārāh* for the Sabbath falling during the festival of Sukkōth; the episode of Joshua and the Angel forms part of the *Haphṭārāh*, also for Passover; the Book of Esther is read on Purim; the narrative of Elijah and the Priests of Baal is the *Haphṭārāh*

[1] Du Mesnil du Buisson, *Revue biblique*, xliii, p. 118.

for the pericope כי תשא (Exod. xxxii–xxxiv); Elisha (*not* Elijah) and the Widow's Child is the lesson for the pericope וירא (Gen. xviii–xxii). Lastly, the Sacrifice of Isaac is the reading from the Pentateuch (Gen. xxii) for the second day of the New Year. This method represents one angle of approach. While, however, it may explain the *raison d'être* of a number of these frescoes, it does not provide the key to them all. Possibly other reasons accounted for the choice of many of these pictures. Certain themes had impressed themselves upon the mind and imagination of the Jewish people from time immemorial. The presence of such heroic figures as Moses, Samuel, David, and Elijah needs no explanation. One explanation for the choice of Ezekiel may be found in the connexion of that prophet with the service in the synagogue, as I have just mentioned. A further reason for the length of wall space it occupies and, consequently, for the importance attached to it, was the absorbing interest which so many of the Jewish communities found in eschatology and in the doctrines of resurrection and immortality, to which the growing mass of apocalyptic literature in the centuries immediately preceding bears so eloquent a tribute. To suggest, as du Mesnil does, that the importance given to the Ezekiel panel was in some respect possibly due to the confusion in the minds of the people at Dura of the Chebar in Babylon with a similarly named river in Syria is little short of fantastic, and argues a profound misunderstanding of the real significance of these pictures.[1]

The Esther panel may have been deliberately placed in that part of the synagogue where it could be seen to the best advantage by the women. For, as I have already mentioned, it was made obligatory upon the women to attend the synagogue on the Feast of Purim, when the Book of Esther was read. It has also been suggested that the fresco illustrating the Unction of David was designedly placed above the seat of honour reserved for Samuel, the archi-

[1] *Revue biblique*, xliii, p. 118.

synagogue, by way of compliment to him for bearing the same name as the prophet.[1]

One source from Jewish literature which may prove helpful in our study of these frescoes, and which appears to have been hitherto overlooked, may be mentioned. I refer to the concluding chapters of Ecclesiasticus (xliv–l), in praise of 'famous men'. Just as Braun found a clue to the subjects of Old Testament illustration in Christian art in the eleventh chapter of the Epistle to the Hebrews, these chapters from the Apocrypha may prove a documentary source of no less value for the choice of themes from the Hebrew Bible in Jewish art. It is remarkable how often these passages from Ecclesiasticus supply a kind of running commentary to the frescoes. Of the worthies portrayed at Dura-Europos, which at the same time form the subject of eulogy in Ecclesiasticus, there are to be mentioned Abraham, Isaac, Jacob, Moses, Aaron, Joshua, Samuel, David, Elijah, and Ezekiel.[2] It is true that Ecclesiasticus has one omission, which in view of the importance assigned to the theme in the synagogue at Dura-Europos, may occasion surprise. Mordecai is not included in the list of 'famous men'. But as the fortunes of Mordecai were inextricably bound up with those of Esther and as the author of Ecclesiasticus omits the mention of women in these chapters (he had no high opinion of them), we are able to understand the reason for such an omission. Moreover, it is well to remember that at the time of the composition of Ecclesiasticus the Book of Esther may not yet have found its way into the canon.

While it would take too long to go through the whole list, a few of the examples of correspondence between the descriptions in Ecclesiasticus and the frescoes of the synagogue may be cited. For example, of Samuel we are told,

'Samuel the prophet of the Lord, beloved of his Lord, established a kingdom, *and anointed princes over his people*.'[3]

---

[1] *Revue biblique*, xliii, p. 558.
[2] I have left out the doubtful pictures from the list.
[3] *Ecclesiasticus*, xlvi. 13 (R.V.).

The last words of this verse, which I have italicized, admirably describe the fresco representing Samuel anointing David.

Another example may be taken from the eulogy upon Elijah:

'Thrice did he thus bring down fire.
How wast thou glorified, O Elijah, in thy wondrous deeds!
And who shall glory like unto thee?
Who did raise up a dead man from death,
And from the place of the dead, by the word of the Most High.'
(xlviii. 3–5: R.V.)

The miracles which are illustrated in the frescoes are thus aptly commemorated in these verses. But it is above all in the description of Aaron the High Priest, and of the High Priest Simon, the son of Onias, officiating in the Temple, that we are provided with a key to the fresco depicting the High Priest. It may be recalled that he is shown in the latter dressed in all the panoply of his priestly vestments and officiating at the sacrifices in the Temple. Both fresco and description serve to emphasize the hold which the ritual of the Temple had obtained over the Jewish mind and the ineffaceable impression it had left upon it. The strangely impressive figure of the High Priest at Dura-Europos forms a fitting complement to the vivid descriptions of the High Priests Aaron and Simon. The following verses from Ecclesiasticus admirably illustrate the subject of the fresco:

'How glorious was he when the people gathered round him
At his coming forth out of the sanctuary!
As the morning star in the midst of a cloud,
As the moon at the full:
As the sun shining forth upon the temple of the Most High,
And as the rainbow giving light in clouds of glory:
As the flower of roses in the days of new *fruits*,
As lilies at the waterspring,
As the shoot of the frankincense tree in the time of summer:
As fire and incense in the censer,
As a vessel all of beaten gold
Adorned with all manner of precious stones:

As an olive tree budding forth fruits,
And as a cypress growing high among the clouds.
When he took up the robe of glory,
And put on the perfection of exultation,
In the ascent of the holy altar,
He made glorious the precinct of the sanctuary.' (l. 5–11; R.V.)

A further clue to the significance of this picture of the High Priest is provided by the service of the synagogue. In the *Mūsāph* service on *Yōm Kippūr* (the Day of Atonement) there are long and elaborate descriptions of the service of the High Priest in the Temple on that day. One of the *piyyūṭīm* in particular, is often little more than a paraphrase of ch. l in Ecclesiasticus.¹ The liturgical usage of the synagogue in later times may thus help us to throw light upon the significance of this fresco in the ancient synagogue at Dura-Europos. How great was the importance attached to the service of the High Priest in the Temple on the Day of Atonement may be gathered from the fact that one tractate of the Talmūdh (the tractate *Yōmā*) is largely devoted to it. In the light of the evidence from the Talmūdh and the liturgy it is perhaps permissible to suggest in this connexion that the Durene fresco illustrates the service of the High Priest on *Yōm Kippūr*, the holiest day in the Jewish year.

Another source which may shed light upon the selection of the subjects in the Durene wall-paintings is provided by the *sᵉlīḥāh* מי שענה, the prototype of the *Ordo Commendationis Animae*, as the late David Kaufmann so brilliantly demonstrated.² It may be recalled that Kaufmann established with equal cogency that the subjects of the paintings on the Christian catacombs corresponded in a remarkable degree to those of the Latin prayer. If we take Kaufmann's arguments a stage further and compare the Hebrew *sᵉlīḥāh*

---

¹ The *piyyūṭ* referred to above is the one beginning כאהל הנמתח בדרי מעלה. It forms part of the Ashkᵉnazzī rite.

² 'Sens et origines des symboles tumulaires dans l'art chrétien primitif', *REJ* xiv. 33–48; 217–53.

with the wall-paintings in the synagogue, we find that at least six of the names and the incidents with which they are connected occur in both. They are, Abraham on Mount Moriah, the Sacrifice of Isaac, the Passage of the Israelites through the Red Sea, Joshua at Gilgal, Elijah on Mount Carmel, and Mordecai and Esther. This number excludes the doubtful attributions. For example, if we accept the identification of one of the frescoes as Jacob's Dream, the number of correspondences is increased to seven. Some of the other incidents mentioned in the *s‘līḥāh* may be equated with the frescoes at Dura, but we cannot be quite sure. However, if the series had been completely preserved it is probable that further parallels would have been discovered. The idea of deliverance in time of trouble is thus one of the principal clues to our understanding of so many of these frescoes, just as it forms the *leitmotiv* in the paintings on the walls of the Christian catacombs.

Another aspect of the subject to which a few words must be devoted is the question whether these frescoes can be reconciled with the edicts of Rabbinic Judaism, or whether they represent a unique phenomenon entirely divorced from its true spirit. The pitfalls that lie in wait for those inadequately equipped in Rabbinic literature are patent when we find a scholar of the eminence of Rostovtzeff stating with almost intimidating professorial finality, 'it is certain that such a decoration of synagogues was never universally adopted as canonical and in conformity with the rules of the Talmud'.[1] We fear that the author has been speaking here without his book. For this statement, made with such dogmatic certitude, is directly refuted by the Talmūdh itself. In the tractate '*Ăbhōdhāh Zārāh* of the Jerusalem Talmūdh we are told,

'In the days of Rabbi Jochanan men began to paint upon the wall, and he did not hinder them.'[2]

[1] *Dura-Europos and its Art*, p. 102.
[2] Fol. 42 *c*, line 4 (Krotoschin edition): ביומוי דרבי יוחנן שרון ציירין על כותלא ולא מחי בידייהו.

THE WALL-PAINTINGS AT DURA-EUROPOS

We have in this *locus classicus* a clear and explicit statement permitting the use of wall-paintings in the synagogue. Rabbi Jochanan bar Nappāḥā, to give him his full name, who permitted this practice, was no insignificant or sectarian Rabbi, but the head of the community in Palestine, whose authority extended far beyond the confines of that country. He was born towards the end of the second century at Sepphoris and died in Tiberias in 279. His date is interesting as his *floruit* covers the period of the second synagogue at Dura. We are thus provided with an approximate *terminus a quo* for the practice of adorning the synagogues with wall-paintings. We are now able to offer an explanation why in the case of the first synagogue the community refrained from making use of representational art, the reason probably being that Rabbinical sanction had not yet been accorded to that form of art in the synagogue. Moreover, these frescoes are thus not to be explained as due to an assertion of religious independence on the part of an isolated Jewish community in Syria. Such painting must have constituted a normal feature of synagogue decoration at the time. There is therefore no reason to suppose that other synagogues may not come to light with wall-paintings similar to those at Dura-Europos, if the same good fortune which attended the discovery of that site could be repeated.[1]

Similarly, when Rostovtzeff remarks,

'It was therefore mere chance that the Jewish community of Dura, which as late as the early third century never thought of decorating their first synagogue with figures of living beings, should in the middle of the third century A.D. have changed their minds and accepted the liberal interpretation of Exodus xx. 4'[2]

---

[1] Coming down to modern times, it is interesting to note that we find wall-paintings in some of the older Polish synagogues. The decoration was restricted to representations of animals like lions, chickens, ducks, and geese, and to landscapes of the Holy Land. The human figure does not appear. Such decoration was, it is hardly necessary to say, quite in harmony with the ordinances of Rabbinical law. See Bruno Italiener, in *Die Darmstädter Pessach-Haggadah*, Leipzig, 1927, p. 17 (Textband).

[2] Op. cit., p. 102.

his statement falls equally wide of the mark. It was not 'mere chance' which induced the Jewish community to take this step, but the clearly expressed sanction of Rabbinic and Talmūdhic law.

Something must now be said of the style and composition of these wall-paintings. Upon this aspect of the subject we cannot do better than quote the authority of Rostovtzeff himself. He says:

'The system of decoration of the synagogue is strikingly similar to that of all the pagan temples of Dura and to that of the Christian Church. In fact, apart from the difference of the subjects one had before one's eyes, on entering the synagogue a decoration exactly like the *naoi* of the temple of the Palmyrene gods and of the temple of Zeus Theos.'[1]

It has been well observed of these paintings that their conception is superior to their execution.[2] In the main, that is a true as well as a wise saying. Certain panels, notably that of Moses reading the Law, reveal a more happy fusion of conception and execution. Some of the frescoes, like the Esther panel, the Discovery of the Infant Moses, Elijah reviving the Widow of Zarephath's Child, convey a sense of dramatic tension and succeed in transcending the technical limitations of the artist. The Ezekiel panel, childishly executed though it be, is redeemed by the strength of the religious emotion which animates it. Some spiritual quality of the living Jewish faith is communicated to many of the wall-paintings which differentiates them from the frescoes in the temples and private houses at Dura-Europos.

The importance of these wall-paintings is twofold. For not only will a study of them throw light upon the subsequent evolution of Jewish iconography, it will also help to determine the relationship of early Christian art to Jewish, and establish the debt which the one owes to the other.

I hope I may be excused for having dealt at such disproportionate length with these obscure and difficult paintings.

[1] Op. cit., p. 114.   [2] *Rep.* vi, p. 382.

THE WALL-PAINTINGS AT DURA-EUROPOS

They have already given rise to an extensive literature, although it is only a few years since they were excavated. When new discoveries are made there is always a danger that the earliest theories and interpretations may be too readily accepted and may even crystallize into a fixed and immutable canon. If I have been compelled to challenge many of the explanations and conclusions first advanced, that is not to depreciate the value and importance of Rostovtzeff and his very able band of collaborators, whose names will always be associated with the wonderful finds uncovered at Dura-Europos. One lesson the paintings reinforce very clearly. They cannot be solved with just an Old Testament in one's hand. One might as well try to read a cuneiform inscription with the help only of a Hebrew dictionary. The paintings must be related to their Jewish background, to the Midhrāsh, the Talmūdh, the apocalyptic literature, the responsa, and kindred works. It is there where we shall find the answer to many of the problems posed by these frescoes.

A word or two must be said of the frescoes recovered from the walls of the neighbouring church at Dura, which dates back some twenty years earlier than the second synagogue. The paintings were there confined to the baptistery only. Two of the extant paintings derive from the Hebrew Bible: Adam and Eve, and David and Goliath. The small range of Old Testament subjects in the church may possibly indicate that Christian art had not yet developed an extensive O. T. picture cycle of its own, but had started hesitatingly to borrow from the Jewish corpus of subjects.

That representations of David and Goliath were common in Talmūdhic times is expressly mentioned by Rashī in his commentary.[1] Similarly, Nathan ben Jehiel in his Talmūdhic lexicon *he-'Ārūkh*, speaks of representations of the Sacrifice of Isaac.[2] We know that in the Middle Ages

---

[1] See Rashī's commentary upon the tractate *Shabbāth* of the Babylonian Talmūdh, fol. 149*a*, s.v. כתב המהלך תחת הצורה ותחת הדיוקנאות

[2] s.v. דיוקן.

wealthy Jews decorated the interior of their houses with scenes from the Hebrew Bible and the outside with secular paintings.[1] This practice may well go back many centuries earlier. In one of the villas excavated at Malta, whose *terminus a quo* may be established from a bust of the Emperor Claudius (A.D. 41–54) found in it, there was discovered a mosaic which it is difficult to interpret as anything else but a representation of Samson and Delila.[2] The mosaic depicts a woman bending over the naked figure of an athlete, clasping his hair with one hand and holding a pair of shears in the other (Pl. XVII). The survival of so early a mosaic depicting a Biblical theme would seem to point to the existence of a Jewish form of Old Testament illustration prior to the earliest products of Christian art. It is natural to suppose that the Jews, with their peculiar receptiveness to their cultural environment, would bring the Hebrew Bible into the service of decoration in emulation and imitation of the current pagan art. Considering that the Hebrew Bible possessed an incomparable repertory of stories, many of them equalling, if not surpassing, the finest tales of classical mythology and peculiarly suited to representation in mosaic and other art-forms, it is not surprising that Jews should have wanted to utilize them for this purpose.

In some ways even more remarkable than the mosaic at Malta is a fresco discovered at Pompeii, which depicts in

[1] I. Abrahams, *Jewish Life in the Middle Ages*, 2nd ed. (1932), p. 162.
[2] Cohn-Wiener, *Die jüdische Kunst*, pp. 105–7. S. Reinach was the first to identify the subject of this mosaic, in the *Revue archéologique*, 1909 (i), pp. 172–3. Rather surprisingly, Reinach did not consider the possibility of the mosaic being a specimen of Jewish art or being connected in any way with Jewish prototypes. He explained its presence in Malta as due instead to Phoenician influence. He suggested that Samson was in some way identified with a local worthy of the name of Meliteus, like the Jewish hero an eater of honey. He thus invested the name with the dual meaning of an inhabitant of Malta and a honey-eater. Reinach's erudite and ingenious explanation postulates too many assumptions for it to be wholly convincing.

caricature the Judgement of Solomon.[1] It is not to be wondered at that its first discoverer should have looked upon it with mingled astonishment and incredulity.[2] Upon a tribunal at which three figures are seated dressed in the Roman garb, the central person is depicted leaning upon his sceptre. Behind these figures stands a group of soldiers. In front of the tribunal, an infant lies stretched upon a table. An executioner, armed with a huge knife, is about to cut the child in two. A woman holds the child down in order to facilitate the execution. Another woman implores the King on her knees to spare the child. The figures are all drawn in caricature.

This fresco does not exhaust the list of subjects drawn from the Hebrew Bible. Another section, forming part of the same series of paintings, depicts a scene by the Nile, with crocodiles swallowing and disgorging pigmies, apparently a variant of the Jonah theme.

These early paintings lend additional point to the possibility of a Jewish picture-cycle of Old Testament illustration existing before the emergence of a similar Christian tradition. In the case of the two paintings at Pompeii it is obvious that there could have been no caricature without previous prototypes to stimulate the mocking spirit of the Graeco-Roman artists. The interesting fact about these three early specimens is that they probably antedate the earliest O. T. illustration by Christian artists. Claudius reigned between A.D. 41 and 54. Pompeii was destroyed in

[1] L. Blau considers it as certain, 'on the basis of the data collected by Juster, *Les Juifs dans l'Empire Romain*, I, 182, n. 11', that 'there were Jews also in Pompeii before the eruption'. See *JQR* N.S., xix, 1928–9, p. 161.

[2] G.-B. de Rossi, who first wrote about it in a letter in the *Bulletin critique*, tome ii, 1882, pp. 272–3. For the literature upon the subject, see *Dictionnaire d'Archéologie chrétienne*, tome 14, s.v. 'Pompéi'. It may be recalled that sacred Christian subjects seem similarly to have become the object of caricature. The graffito (early third century?), found in the Domus Gelotiana on the Palatine Hill at Rome has been claimed as a caricature of the crucified Christ. See s.v. 'Âne', op. cit. But, as Dr. Kurz informs me, this graffito is ripe for a fresh investigation.

A.D. 79. Even allowing for the latest possible dates for the mosaic and caricatures, we are, I think, justified in claiming for them that they represent the earliest surviving examples of Old Testament illustration, Christian or Jewish.[1] This brings us to the question of the origin of Christian art, a consideration of which must, however, be deferred to the concluding chapter. Here it need only be said that if Jewish picture-cycles of the Old Testament were already in existence, then a strong case can be made out for the early Christians drawing upon them. For it would be going against human nature to imagine that the early Christians would go to the trouble of creating a new repertory of their own when they could find to hand ready-made material.

Compared with the Durene frescoes, the other extant archaeological material bearing on the subject is of relatively lesser importance, although not without considerable historical value. The most interesting remains are those in the ancient synagogues of Palestine, like Bēth-Alphā, Jerash and Naʿaran, and those of of Greece and North Africa. Fortunately, a previous lecturer in this series, E. L. Sukenik, has dealt fully with the synagogues of Palestine and Greece. There is therefore no need for me to traverse the same ground. The most striking of the discoveries was a fifth-century mosaic floor found at Bēth-Alphā in 1928.[2] This mosaic was divided into three registers and contained an interesting if crudely executed collection of Biblical motifs (Pl. XVIII). The bottom register illustrates the Sacrifice of Isaac, with more amplitude of detail than the corresponding painting at Dura. On the left, the ass and two servants of Abraham are to be observed. On the right we have a representation of Abraham about to slay Isaac, and in the centre, the ram caught in a tree. The hand of God appears above Abraham.

The objects in the middle register do not really concern

---

[1] The significance of the Samson and Delila mosaic found at Malta and of the two caricature paintings at Pompeii will be discussed further in the concluding chapter.

[2] See E. L. Sukenik, *Ancient Synagogues in Palestine and Greece*, pp. 32–5.

THE WALL-PAINTINGS AT DURA-EUROPOS 63

us. So we pass on to the register above it. Here are depicted with the same crudity and *naïveté* as distinguish the two other compartments, a characteristic collection of objects, most of them familiar to us from other sources. In the centre is a representation of a Tōrāh shrine, guarded on each side by a lion. At either end of the pediment is perched a large plump bird, probably an ostrich, the symbol of righteousness and truth. These birds are probably one of the conventional forms of representing the cherubim.[1] A Menōrāh stands on each side of the Tōrāh shrine. Hanging down by rings from the top of the frame of the fresco are curtains, drawn back, and provided with cords to which a weight is attached at the end. The vacant spaces are filled in with representations, in pairs, one on each side of the Ark of the Covenant, of the *shōphār*, the *lūlābh* and *ethrīgh*, and the snuff-dishes. Less familiar objects are the flowering rod of Aaron on the right of the Ark, and the barren rod on the left. Both these rods are depicted in the shape of trees, that of Aaron having a bird perched on the top bough. According to Christian legend—as found, for example, in the Syriac 'Book of the Bee'—Aaron's staff is a fragment of the Tree of Knowledge. The form in which Aaron's rod is here depicted has led a recent art student to connect it with the Tree of Life, owing to its affinities with earlier examples illustrating the same theme.[2] The theme of the flowering rod had a great attraction for the medieval mind, as can be seen, for example, from the legends of Tannhäuser, the Virgin Mary and her suitors, and the miracles of St. Ninian.

The Ark of the Covenant, the Tabernacle and its sacred vessels are often depicted in Christian illuminated Bibles and other classes of manuscripts. The Epistle to the Hebrews ix. 1–5 reflects the interest in the subject. While

[1] Dr. Z. Ameisenowa is not quite correct in asserting (in 'The Tree of Life', p. 342, note 1), 'Philo speaks explicitly of the Cherubim as birds'. Philo (*De Vita Mosis*, II. xx, Loeb edition) speaks of them as πτηνά, which refers to any winged creatures, not necessarily birds (ὄρνιθες).   [2] Z. Ameisenowa, 'The Tree of Life', p. 344.

these sacred objects can usually be immediately recognized, they may sometimes be difficult to identify. For example, the Syriac Biblical manuscript, of the seventh century (if not earlier), which Omont has described, contains several single 'portraits' of the Prophets, standing in front of a portico. Two of these porticoes are distinguished by having figures of birds on the pediment and by a curtain hanging down from it. May we not read into this representation, in view of the birds (a form of the cherubim?), and the curtain (intended for the *pārōkheth*?), a picture of the Holy of Holies or the Ark of the Covenant (Pl. xix. 1)?[1] The more famous Ashburnham Pentateuch contains a frontispiece whose Jewish character has only been recognized in recent years, in an article by J. C. Sloane (Pl. xix. 2).[2] He claims that the frontispiece is a representation of a Tōrāh shrine.[3] It is, however, more likely to be a copy of the Ark of the Covenant. There would be no point in a Christian artist painting a piece of synagogue furniture like the Tōrāh shrine. The difficulties vanish, however, if we identify the object as the Ark of the Covenant. For, as we have just seen, the Tabernacle and its sacred vessels appear frequently in illuminated Christian manuscripts.

Other themes depicted in the mosaics of the ancient synagogues of Palestine are a version of Noah and his family entering the Ark, together with the animals, found in Jerash; and the story of Daniel in the lions' den, the latter discovered at Na'aran. It need hardly be mentioned that both these themes are a commonplace of Christian art. One other ancient synagogue, not described by Sukenik, as it falls outside the scope of his book, merits

---

[1] 'Peintures de l'Ancien Testament dans un manuscrit syriaque du viie ou viiie siècle,' Paris, 1909.

[2] H. Leclercq, for example, dismisses the frontispiece as unworthy of an extended notice, not appreciating its real significance. See *Dictionnaire d'Archéologie chrétienne*, vol. i, part 2, col. 2971.

[3] J. C. Sloane in *JQR* n.s., xxv (1934), pp. 1–12.

a few words. I refer to the synagogue of Ḥammām Lif, near Carthage.[1] Its well-executed fifth-century mosaic floor contains a number of motifs drawn from the Hebrew Bible interwoven with later eschatological material. The central section of the mosaic is divided into two panels (Pl. xx. 1). The upper compartment depicts the Messianic life. Unfortunately, the left portion of this picture is damaged. The horned head is all that remains of what was most probably a representation of Behemoth, whose flesh was reserved for the righteous in Paradise. Other items of the Messianic feast are visible: the monster Leviathan, with his mate; and the geese, whose presence we have already noted in the central panel of the frescoes at Dura. The lower compartment introduces us to the Fountain of Life, at whose edge are perched two peacocks, the symbols of immortality. To the left and right of the fountain are placed two trees, one almost certainly the Tree of Life, the other possibly the Tree of Knowledge. A (presumably) Christian mosaic of the sixth century, also from Carthage, now in the British Museum, provides an interesting parallel (Pl. xx. 2).[2] In this we are shown two stags drinking from a fountain.[3] Over the heads of the stags hover two very plump birds. On either side of the fountain are young trees. The affinities between the two mosaics are fairly obvious, but their mutual relationships and interdependence have yet to be worked out. Here it is sufficient to say that while these familiar motifs of the 'fountain of life' and the 'tree of life' depicted upon Christian mosaics and frescoes are more immediately derived from the vision of 'a new heaven and a new earth' in Revelation xxi, the source for these symbolical conceptions must be sought in the Hebrew Bible.

[1] See F. M. Biebel, 'The Mosaics of Hammam Lif', *Art Bulletin*, 1936, pp. 541–51; also Z. Ameisenowa, 'The Tree of Life', p. 334.

[2] See Dalton, *Guide*, 1929, pp. 78–9 and fig. 49.

[3] The background to this symbolical representation is provided by Psalm xlii. 1 ('As the hart panteth after the water brooks, so panteth my soul after thee, O God').

CHAPTER III
THE ILLUMINATED HEBREW BIBLES OF THE EAST

THIS concludes our brief survey of the archaeological material extant. We enter into more peaceful country, where the serene landscape is scarcely ruffled by the rude winds of controversy, when we turn to a consideration of the illuminated manuscripts themselves. At the very outset we are struck by the rigidly demarcated categories into which copies of the Hebrew Bible divide themselves. These categories may be conveniently described as ritual and secular, or, if you like, public and private. Rabbinical Judaism has minutely regulated every detail connected with the copying of the Pentateuch and other portions of the Hebrew Bible required for the service of the synagogue. The quality of the parchment, the height and width of the column, the amount of text in each line—all these and many other particulars must conform to carefully formulated laws. The text must be free of all ornament, unless the *Tāghīn* (the crowns on certain of the letters) could be considered as such. No notes of any kind are admitted; no vowels, accents, or, excepting the *puncta extraordinaria*, other orthographic devices. Moreover, such texts could only be written in rolls, the book-form being prohibited.[1] The *textus receptus* must be copied by the scribe with the most scrupulous fidelity and accuracy. It is then carefully corrected and collated according to the manuals of the scribes.

Such are the rules that govern the ritual copies of the Hebrew Bible. But while Rabbinical Judaism jealously guarded the transcribing of these manuscripts, it imposed no such rigid uniformity and austerity upon codices made for private individuals. Here a good deal of latitude was allowed, which made possible the subsequent development of artistically produced Hebrew Bibles. It is with this latter cate-

[1] The Samaritans similarly eschew any form of ornament in their copies of the Pentateuch.

gory of Hebrew Bibles that we are here concerned. We cannot say how far back in the Middle Ages the Jews first practised the art of illumination—as distinct from the gold and silver writing mentioned in the Letter of Aristeas and in the Talmūdh and Midhrāsh. The earliest examples of Hebrew illuminated Bibles hail from the East. As we should expect, the decoration often reflects the styles prevalent in Muslim countries. Representational art is—as in the case of illuminated Kur'āns—rigidly excluded. Only decorative patterns are introduced. While human beings or animals are eschewed, there appears to have been no objection against the representation of the Tabernacle or Temple and the sacred vessels. Leningrad possesses fragments of a Pentateuch, bearing a date corresponding to A.D. 930, which, besides being the earliest dated illuminated Hebrew Bible, shows interesting and characteristic forms of decoration of various kinds.[1] One page contains a representation of the Temple and its sacred vessels. It is instructive to see how the problem of representational art was handled. The Cherubim over the Mercy Seat have disappeared, their place being taken by foliage patterns (Pl. XXI). Jewish art, or possibly, in this case, Ḳaraite, is thus seen to adapt itself to the exigencies of Muslim law and practice.

The custom of reproducing the sacred vessels of the Tabernacle or Temple finds a curious parallel in the Samaritan sect. One of the plates in the late Dr. Gaster's Schweich Lectures on the Samaritans shows us a picture of the vessels of the Tabernacle, with descriptions in Samaritan.[2] It is a rough drawing made in blue chalk upon the metal case which is used for holding the special scroll of the Samaritan Pentateuch exhibited during the service. In addition to the vessels like the Golden Menōrāh, the Table of the Showbread, the trumpets, &c., we find a representation of the Cherubim over the Mercy Seat, flanked on

[1] Cod. II. 17. Reproduced in Stassoff and Günzburg, L'Ornement hébreu.

[2] *The Samaritans*, London, 1925, pl. 4. A note on this illustration is found on pp. 193–4.

68   ILLUMINATED HEBREW BIBLES OF THE EAST

either side by a budding and barren rod (Pl. xxii). The budding rod is here described as the 'rod of Moses', whereas the barren rod is called the 'rod of Aaron'.[1] According to Gaster, this case is a late copy made in the seventeenth century, but it is claimed by the Samaritans to be a reproduction of an earlier specimen made in silver, which was stolen from them by the Arabs in Shechem.

The next specimen, which, though undated, also probably belongs to the tenth century, shows once again how deeply penetrated Jewish decoration in the East was by Muslim art.[2] This page of a Hebrew Bible written in Egypt might, excepting for the Hebrew text, well come from an illuminated copy of the Ḳur'ān (Pl. xxiii. 1). The close resemblance of this Bible to copies of the sacred book of the Muslims, points, perhaps, to a Ḳaraite origin. For it was the Ḳaraite sect rather than the Rabbinic Jews who absorbed so much of Arabic culture. They had, in fact, so thoroughly assimilated the Arabic language in Egypt and Palestine that they even wrote their Hebrew Bibles in some cases in the Arabic script, thus reversing the custom and practice of the Rabbinic Jews, who went to the other extreme of writing their Arabic in Hebrew characters.

The British Museum possesses a fragment of an illuminated copy of the Book of Exodus, which provides an additional proof of the progressive Arabicization of that sect.[3] Only the first twenty-one leaves, containing the text of chap. i–viii, have survived.[4] The manuscript is written in Arabic characters, the Hebrew text having been transcribed in that form. The Hebrew vowel points and accents may have been added later. These accretions invest the manuscript with a curiously hybrid appearance. The text

[1] Jewish tradition identifies Aaron's rod with that of Moses.

[2] Leningrad, Cod. II. 49. Reproduced in Stassoff and Günzburg.

[3] The Ḳaraite Judah Mē'īr, for example, speaks of himself and his fellow-countrymen as belonging to the גמאעה אלמסתערב ('the Arabicized community'). See G. Margoliouth, *Cat. Heb. MSS.* part i, p. 194.

[4] A facsimile and full description of this manuscript (Or. 2540) are given in R. Hoerning's *British Museum Karaite MSS.*

ILLUMINATED HEBREW BIBLES OF THE EAST 69

is preceded by two handsome full-page illuminations in gold and brownish tints (Pl. XXIII. 2). In addition, the spaces marking the $p^e th\bar{u}h\bar{o}th$ and $s^e th\bar{u}m\bar{o}th$ (the open and closed sections) are filled in with gold ornamentation. The manuscript is unfortunately not dated, but has been assigned on palaeographical grounds to the tenth century.

Two other fragments of Hebrew illuminated Bibles, which may be attributed to the same century, have been described by the late Dr. Gaster, to whom they belonged before they were acquired by the British Museum.[1] Both these codices, respectively numbered 150 and 151, have gold illumination. Codex 150 originally contained the whole of the Pentateuch. Though much ravaged by time and rough treatment, it still bears traces of its pristine handsomeness. Each page is enclosed in a gold-ruled frame (Pl. XXIV. 1). The text is divided into three gold-ruled columns, the margins thus formed being given over to the Māsōrāh Parva and to decorations in the form of gold rosettes. The same rosettes are to be found within the columns, noticeably in the spaces traditionally left open. The Māsōrāh Magna is to be found on the upper and lower margins of the page, where it almost always appears in manuscripts of the Hebrew Bible. The rosettes and other forms of decoration employed betray marked affinities with the style of illuminated Ḳur'āns. Nevertheless, they harmonize admirably with the Hebrew text.

The other manuscript formerly in the possession of Dr. Gaster consists of fragments of a codex of the Hagiographa. Here the style of illumination is noticeably different from the fragment of the illuminated Pentateuch. The designs are bold rather than beautiful. The delicately executed rosettes are for the most part replaced by small roughly drawn circles filled in with gold. This form of decoration is interspersed with rather coarse chain-like ornamentations (Pl. XXIV. 2). It is possible that the manuscript was not in

[1] *Hebrew Illuminated Bibles of the IXth and Xth Centuries*, London, 1901. The manuscripts are now numbered Or. 9879 and 9880.

the first place illuminated but that these decorations are later accretions. This question, like so many other aspects connected with the subject of illumination in Hebrew manuscripts, awaits a careful study. The provenance of both these manuscripts is the East, but here again it would be rash in our present state of knowledge of the subject to state confidently their more precise locality.

Two Hebrew Bibles in the British Museum, which have been assigned to the eleventh or twelfth century, deserve a brief notice. They both appear to belong to the same school. Each of them contains a copy of the Pentateuch, accompanied by the Aramaic version (*Targūm*) attributed to Onkᵉlōs. The punctuation is of the superlinear type. The first of these, Or. 2363, is more complete than its fellow, Or. 1467. Written upon vellum, it is remarkable for its ornamentation, which plainly shows the source of inspiration for the beautiful Spanish Hebrew Bibles of the fourteenth and fifteenth centuries.[1] In this manuscript the ornamentation is far more restricted, being confined to the beginning of each pericope, the end of each Book of the Pentateuch, and to the two Songs of Moses (Exod. xv and Deut. xxxii). The decoration is executed in coloured inks, red, green, and yellow being used. The beginning of each pericope is indicated in the column by the initial פ (for פרשה) surmounted by a budding tree. This motif is perhaps to be identified with the Tree of Life as symbolizing the Tōrāh. The illuminated Ḳur'āns, it may be recalled, exemplify a similar if more conventionalized form of ornamentation, to which the Muslims give the name *shujair* ('little tree'). Each book of the Pentateuch closes with an ornamental frame containing borders of chain and leaf ornamentation in colours. The centre of the frame contains the Masoretic rubric giving the number of verses contained in the book.

[1] For descriptions of these two manuscripts see G. Margoliouth, *Catalogue of Hebrew and Samaritan Manuscripts in the British Museum*, part i, 1901, pp. 39–41 (nos. 65–6).

ILLUMINATED HEBREW BIBLES OF THE EAST

The two Songs of Moses are marked out for more elaborate decoration. The first is enclosed by ornamented borders of chain and scroll work, which still bear traces of their former impressiveness, although the passage of time has dealt harshly with them. The second Song of Moses is embellished in addition with rosettes and the hexagram called *Māghēn Dāvīdh* ('Shield of David') in the blank space between the two columns. Although for the most part soberly transcribed, the Māsōrāh in this MS. is occasionally arranged in geometrical patterns of not too extravagant shapes.

The other manuscript, Or. 1467, more fragmentary than the first and also written upon vellum, exemplifies the same form of decoration. The style of the writing of both the manuscripts is described by Margoliouth as belonging to the Babylonian or Persian type.[1] It seems also to show affinities with the Yemenite hand, but that may possibly be due to the fact that the form of Hebrew writing current in Persia influenced the Yemenite scribes.

This brings our summary account of the Hebrew Bibles of the East to a close. Owing to the bad preservation and fragmentary nature of many of these copies the place which the artistic Hebrew Bible of the East occupies in the history of illuminated Hebrew manuscripts cannot be easily defined. There can be little doubt that the East influenced materially the development of the art of Hebrew illumination in the West, but the subject calls for a closer organization of the material available before important positive results can be reached. A cursory examination of some of these Eastern manuscripts, notably Or. 2363, reveals striking points of contact with the Spanish and Portuguese Hebrew Bibles of two centuries later. This is not surprising in view of the strong cultural and religious links which bound the Jews of the West to the East. But it must be left for further research to define the relationship between the Hebrew illuminated Bibles of the East and those of the Iberian peninsula more closely and clearly.

[1] Op. cit., pp. 39*a*, 40*b*.

CHAPTER IV

THE ILLUMINATED MANUSCRIPTS OF THE WEST

THE illuminated Hebrew Bibles of the West fall roughly into the two divisions of representational and non-representational art. The latter category far outnumbers the former. Indeed, the number of extant illustrated Hebrew Bibles is extremely small. One of the earliest of such copies, and certainly by far the finest, is the British Museum MS. Additional 11639. The volume is not actually dated, but from the inclusion of calendar tables beginning with the year corresponding to A.D. 1277–8, we may reasonably assign that date as the approximate time of the transcription and illumination of the manuscript. Strictly speaking, the claim of the manuscript to be considered an illuminated Hebrew Bible may be challenged. The volume is far more than that. Apart from the Pentateuch, the Psalms, the *Haphṭārōth,* and other portions of the Hebrew Bible, it consists of copious selections from the liturgy as well as a mass of miscellaneous literature. It could therefore be more aptly described as a collectaneous volume. However, from the fact that it contains some two-score full-page illuminations forming a kind of picture-cycle of the Old Testament, we are, I think, fully justified in treating it as an illustrated Hebrew Bible, more particularly as it is clear that the owner himself regarded it in that light, when he incorporated these four sets of illuminations into the volume. The provenance of the manuscript is Northern France. It consists of over 700 leaves of the finest vellum, apart from the forty miniatures, which are painted upon a thicker quality of parchment. In size it is a small quarto. It is written in a French square and Rabbinic character, mainly in black, but sometimes in yellow and red ink, and, very occasionally, in gold. With the exception of the last 300 folios, which are devoid of ornament of any kind, almost every leaf is em-

ILLUMINATED MANUSCRIPTS OF THE WEST 73

bellished with some decoration or another. The profusion and excellence of the ornamentation is remarkable. The manuscript is lavishly provided with initials illuminated in gold, and with beautifully executed figures of animals of various kinds, grotesques, shields, coats of arms, and other patterns, the artist everywhere displaying great resourcefulness, variety, and superb skill. But even more interesting from the point of view of these lectures are the numerous full-page miniatures forming a repertory of Old Testament illustration. In style they remind us of the best work of the contemporary French schools. The miniatures exhibit many interesting features. In the first place it seems highly probable that they were not executed by the same artist who was responsible for the illuminations accompanying the text. The parchment upon which these miniatures are painted is thicker and darker in colour, its edges projecting slightly from the rest of the volume. We may therefore legitimately deduce that they were ordered separately and afterwards inserted in different parts of the manuscript. The miniatures, too, follow no chronological order, with the exception of five in the last set (nos. 1–3, 5–6) and nos. 7–10 in the first set, both of which depict the same themes and are arranged in the same order. The lack of chronological sequence in the rest of the miniatures is very marked. We find, for example, a picture of David playing the harp followed by a representation of Abraham welcoming the three angels.

The miniatures are for the most part accompanied by descriptions in Hebrew.[1] These are in several cases ungrammatical. Some of the descriptions in the fourth and last set are now almost illegible. Furthermore, it appears to have been so far overlooked that the descriptions in the fourth set have been added in a later Italian hand and, what is more important, are, in two instances, wrong.

[1] The miniature of Daniel in the presence of Darius (upper compartment of fol. 260a), like that of the High Priest on fol. 523a, has no inscription. The legends in Hebrew accompanying the miniatures are transcribed in Margoliouth's *Catalogue*.

The following is a description of the miniatures in the order of their appearance.[1]

First Series

1. Fol. 114a. The Menōrāh, painted in gold, on a ground of green, blue, and red. On the left, Aaron the High Priest pouring oil into the lamps (Pl. xxv. 1).[2]
2. Fol. 115a. This miniature has hardly any relevance to Old Testament illustration, but is interesting as revealing a taste for the occult sciences so characteristic of the Middle Ages. It shows the palm of the hand, with notes on palmistry written across it.
3. Fol. 116a. According to the accompanying Hebrew description, this miniature represents King Solomon reading the Tōrāh. The volume he is reading is a book and not, as Margoliouth incorrectly describes it, a scroll.[3] Across the book is written תורת משה ('the Law of Moses'), in gold letters. Instead of a crown, as we should expect if he were a king, the figure wears a red cap. This unexpected headgear raises doubts as to the correctness of the Hebrew description underneath the miniature. Does this miniature possibly represent Moses reading the Law? Such an explanation would account for the wearing of a cap instead of a crown more satisfactorily. More point is given to this interpretation if we recall that the book which the figure is reading is described as the 'Law of Moses'. Moreover, representations of Solomon reading the Law are unusual. The figure is seated on a chair, his feet resting on a footstool. The miniature is enclosed in a vaulted portico.
4. Fol. 117b. King David, wearing a crown and playing upon a harp. The whole enclosed in an arch.
5. Fol. 118a. In two compartments. (i) Abraham rising from his chair at the entrance to his tent to greet the three angels. (ii) Abraham and his guests seated round a table with various

---

[1] For an account of these miniatures, see the *Catalogue of the Hebrew and Samaritan Manuscripts in the British Museum*, by G. Margoliouth, part iii, no. 1056 (pp. 423–6), upon which I have drawn freely.

[2] The High Priest wears no mitre but the characteristic peaked cap worn by the Jews in the Middle Ages.

[3] See Margoliouth's *Catalogue*, l.c., p. 423, col. 1. Margoliouth does not challenge the correctness of the Hebrew description underneath the miniature.

kinds of food upon it. The broad shade of the terebinth of Mamre shelters them from the heat of the sun.

6. Fol. 118*b*. In two compartments. (i) Sarah in her tent, with the angel questioning Abraham and pointing in her direction.[1] (ii) On the right, an angel announcing to Abraham that Sarah would have a son. On the left, the other two angels leaving on their mission of destruction.[2]

7. Fol. 119*a*. The miniature is divided into two equal sections by perpendicular lines of gold, each section representing an angel casting fire and brimstone upon a city. According to the Hebrew inscription underneath, the miniature represents the destruction of Sodom by the two angels (זה סדום כאשר הפכו אותה המלאכים—'This is Sodom after the angels had destroyed it'.) But the symmetrical division of the miniature into two sections, the second being a duplication of the first, makes it probable that the destruction of the *two* cities of Sodom and Gomorra was thereby intended (Pl. XXVI. 1).[3]

8. Fol. 119*b*. In two compartments. (i) The two angels leading Lot and his two daughters away from the city. On the right, Lot's wife, remaining behind and looking back, is turned into a pillar of salt. (ii) Lot with his two daughters in the cave.

9. Fol. 120*a*. The passage of the Israelites through the Red Sea. Moses holds his rod aloft in his right hand whilst carrying the Tables of the Law in his left, the latter detail an unconsciously proleptic touch on the part of the artist. The Children of Israel pass unscathed through the waves. At each top corner appears an angel, surrounded by a screen of flame. It was the duty of these angels to stand between the Egyptian hosts and the camp of Israel.

10. Fol. 120*b*. In two compartments. (i) Moses striking the Rock. The figure next to him is probably Aaron. (ii) The Brazen

---

[1] Margoliouth's description of this scene (l.c., p. 423, col. 2) as 'Sarah in the tent with Abraham pointing towards the same by way of informing the angel', requires correction. Abraham is clearly indicated by his Jewish cap.

[2] According to Rabbinic tradition an angel is not entrusted with more than one task. That is why three angels were sent, one to announce the birth of a son to Sarah, another to destroy the city of Sodom, and the third (Raphael) to heal Abraham's circumcision. See Rashi's commentary on Genesis xviii. 2.

[3] Margoliouth (l.c., p. 423, col. 2) does not question the accuracy of the accompanying Hebrew inscription.

Serpent, set high on a column, with tongues of flame shooting from his mouth. Below, a group of Israelites in attitude of supplication to the reptile.

11. Fol. 121a. In two compartments. (i) Judith standing before Holofernes, who is seated and wears a crown. (ii) Judith cutting off the head of Holofernes. Apocryphal subjects, it may be noted, are extremely rare in Jewish iconography, in contrast to their fairly frequent appearance in Christian illuminated manuscripts. Whether the inclusion of this miniature (as well as others) points to Christian influence—as it well may—is a subject worth investigating. The lack of chronological sequence which distinguishes the majority of these miniatures is illustrated by the next picture.

12. Fol. 121b. In two compartments. (i) Aaron the High Priest burning incense on the golden altar. (ii) The Sea of Solomon's Temple, suspended upon the backs of two lions. This version thus differs from the account in 1 Kings vii. 25, where the animals are said to be oxen.

13. Fol. 122a. The final miniature in this series, which is full-page, portrays the Tree of Life, with four angels guarding it, each holding a long, glittering lance in his hand.

Second Series

The second series is an extremely short one, consisting of only three miniatures, the space reserved for the fourth having been left blank.

1. Fol. 259b. This is the only miniature to be divided into four compartments, although the episodes depicted are actually only two. (i–ii) Nebuchadnezzar calling upon the three noble youths, Hananiah, Mishael, and Azariah to worship this golden image. (iii–iv) The three youths in the fiery furnace, with the archangel Gabriel between them. Left, Nebuchadnezzar, with his counsellors, gazing with astonishment upon them.

2. Fol. 260a. In two compartments. (i) Daniel in the presence of Darius. (ii) The prophet in the lions' den.

3. Fol. 260b. Ahasuerus, seated upon his throne, extending his sceptre to Esther.

Third Series

1. Fol. 516b. A figure formed of three concentric circles, containing the names of the signs of the zodiac in the outer circle, and the names of the Hebrew months and those of the seven planets respectively in the two inner circles. All the names are written

ILLUMINATED MANUSCRIPTS OF THE WEST 77

in letters of gold. The conventional representations of the signs of the zodiac are absent. This and the next miniature thus reflect the current fashions of the Christian illuminated manuscripts in which this subject figures so frequently. To what extent these two miniatures are to be linked up with the deep Jewish interest in the planets and the seasons, which the fifth-century mosaic at Bēth-Alphā so strikingly exemplifies, is another question.

2. Fol. 517a. Another circular figure, with the sun, moon, and stars painted upon it.
3. Fol. 517b. A picture of a large bird, looking somewhat like an ostrich, executed in vivid colours of scarlet and blue, with a huge egg underneath it. The artist has here drawn upon Rabbinic legend for his subject. According to the inscription it is a representation of the fabulous bird known to the Talmūdh as בר־יוכני (Bar-Yokhnī).[1]
4. Fol. 518a. The Judgement of Solomon. The king is seated on his throne, wearing a crown and holding his sceptre in his right hand. To the right, a soldier is about to execute the king's judgement. On the left, the real mother begs the king to spare the child, whilst the false claimant is cleverly depicted in an attitude of expectant triumph.
5. Fol. 518b. The Leviathan.
6. Fol. 519a. The fabulous beast known to the Rabbis as the שור הבר (Shōr hab-bār). According to the Talmūdh it is apparently a kind of buffalo. The inclusion of representations of these three fabulous animals raises the question of their relationship to the medieval bestiaries.[2] In this connexion it may not

[1] 'These [ostrich] eggs had been frequent ornaments in Mohammedan mosques; crusaders brought them home, and by this time they were sometimes hung in Christian Churches. In Durandus's *Rationale Divinorum Officiorum* fantastic reasons are suggested for the presence of such eggs in churches. The contemporary Archbishop Pecham suggests another and more natural symbolical explanation: ostrich eggs are hung up in churches and placed before the eyes for this reason, to warn them against imitating ostriches in their carelessness for their young.' See G. G. Coulton, *Art and the Reformation*, p. 255, from which I have quoted the above, partly in an abridged form. A bird with a cone (? egg) appears to be represented on the (first) clay tablet from Gezer, of about the 'Amarna stratum'. See S. A. Cook, op. cit., pp. 100–1.

For the Talmūdhic references to the Bar-Yokhnī, see the tractates of the Babylonian Talmūdh *Yōmā* 80a and *Sukkāh* 5b.

[2] Another illuminated Hebrew Bible containing illustrations from

be inappropriate to recall that a Jewish origin has recently been sought for the famous *Physiologus*, the parent of the medieval bestiaries. It has been suggested that Physiologus conceals the identity of King Solomon himself, whom Jewish legend—to be followed afterwards by Christian and Mohammedan—had endowed with dominion over the animal world and knowledge of their speech.[1] The juxtaposition of illustrations of these fabulous animals to a representation of King Solomon may thus be due to design rather than accident.

7. Fol. 519b. The budding staff of Aaron in the centre, flanked on each side by the eleven barren staves of the princes of the tribes. The staff of Aaron is here shown as a large tree, with three boughs covered with white blossom. The continuity of Jewish iconography is illustrated once more by a theme made so familiar to us from the early monuments of Jewish religious art, like the mosaic at Bēth-Alphā, for example.[2]

8. Fol. 520a. Samson rending the lion. Samson kneels one leg upon the back of the animal, and rends his jaws with his hands. The lion is vigorously drawn, a touch of extravagance being provided by a three-tufted tail of preternatural length.

9. Fol. 520b. A charming miniature representing Adam on the right, and on the left, Eve, with the Tree of Knowledge between them, round which is entwined the serpent, the latter depicted with the head of a child. This peculiar form of representing the serpent is recalled in the famous lines by Pope upon Lord Harvey from the *Epistle to Arbuthnot*:

> *Eve's* tempter thus the Rabbins have exprest,
> A Cherub's face, a reptile all the rest.[3]

a bestiary, also of French origin, and assigned by the author of the article to the thirteenth century, is described by Z. Ameisenowa (in Polish) in *Miesięcznik Żydowski*, Warsaw, 1933. For the reference to the *Shōr hab-bār*, see the tractate of the Babylonian Talmūdh *Hullīn* 80a.

[1] See R. Wischnitzer-Bernstein, *Gestalten und Symbole der jüdischen Kunst*, Berlin, 1935, p. 150.

[2] The history of the diffusion of this theme in Christian legend lies outside the scope of our subject.

[3] See Kaufmann, op. cit., pp. 261–2, for a similar representation of the serpent. The Hebrew Bible, MS. Casanatense no. 283, in a full-page illustration of the same theme, has the serpent painted with a female head, with long golden hair, a manner of presentation also found in Christian manuscripts. See R. Gottheil, *JQR* xvii (1905), 652.

ILLUMINATED MANUSCRIPTS OF THE WEST

10. Fol. 521*a*. Noah's Ark. In contrast with the naïve charm of the preceding miniature this appears unexciting. The patriarch is seen stretching out his hand from the window to bring the dove into the ark. She is depicted with an olive leaf in her beak. A raven is perched on the top of the ark.
11. Fol. 521*b*. The Sacrifice of Isaac. An angel appears from the sky. He catches hold of Abraham's raised knife with his right hand, pointing with his left to the ram caught in the bush by its horns. Isaac lies upon a high golden altar. He is partially bound, his left hand being tied to his foot. He is painted very small in comparison with the gigantic height of his father. A bundle of faggots rests by the altar and to the left of it. The theme of synagogue frescoes and mosaics thus reappears in the pages of a Hebrew illuminated Bible. Its appeal was unfailing to Jew and Christian alike, although its interest for the latter was to some extent typological, as prefiguring the Crucifixion (Pl. xxv. 2).[1]
12. Fol. 522*a*. The Cherubim over the Mercy Seat. Underneath is the golden Table of the Showbread. To the right, a golden censer (Pl. xxvi. 2). It is possible to detect some kind of sequence in this and the next two miniatures, as they all three illustrate the service of the High Priest.
13. Fol. 522*b*. The High Priest and the Golden Menōrāh. Aaron, with a red cap on his head, pours oil into the lamps. This miniature duplicates the theme of the very first illustration in the first series, to which it is similar in treatment, if not in detail. It is not easy to explain this repetition except on the assumption that more than one artist was employed on these sets. Even to an untrained eye they appear to exemplify different styles.
14. Fol. 523*a*. The last of the three miniatures which have for their subject the High Priesthood and the Tabernacle with its sacred objects has in it some elements of mystery. The subject is clear enough. In the centre is a figure in the vestments of a High Priest, no doubt intended to represent Aaron. He wears the breast-plate of judgement. The skirts of his robes are adorned with bells. Instead of a mitre, which we should expect,

[1] How widely disseminated Christian paintings of this subject had become in his day is attested by Augustine (354–430) in his polemic *Contra Faustum* (xxii. 73: 'factum ita nobile ut tot linguis cantatum, tot locis pictum et aures et oculos dissimulantis feriret'.) Other Fathers of the Church, notably Gregory of Nyssa, Ephraim, and Cyril of Alexandria, confirm the evidence of Augustine.

he wears a crown, upon which are inscribed the words קדש ליהוה ('Holy unto the Lord').[1] It is possible that the artist refrained from painting a mitre for Aaron, as that article of headgear was peculiarly associated with the high dignitaries of the Christian Church. On the left of the High Priest is a figure in an attitude of supplication, and, on the right, a figure in a similar posture holding in his hands an object upon which the words אורים ותמים ('Urim and Thummim') are inscribed. The miniature is, therefore, apparently intended to represent a consultation of the oracle. It is to be noted that the High Priest does not actually wear the Urim and Thummim, unless it is supposed that they are being handed to him to put on (Pl. xxvii. 1).

15. Fol. 523*b*. David and Goliath, so favourite a subject of Christian iconography. The towering bulk of Goliath armed *cap à pied*, and holding a huge lance in his left hand and his shield in his right, faces the diminutive figure of David, who is unarmed and whose only weapon is a sling. In his right hand he holds his shepherd's crook. A small dog barks at Goliath, while rams and sheep unconcernedly crop the pasture by the side of David.[2]

16. Fol. 524*a*. Esther pleading before Ahasuerus. The theme is illustrated here for the second time. It is first found in miniature 3 of the second series.

17. Fol. 525*b*. Moses praying for victory, his hands supported by Aaron and Hur. This is another favourite theme of Christian artists, where it figures as a type of the cross.

18. Fol. 526*a*. Samuel slaying Agag.

19. Fol. 527*b*.[3] Mordecai and Haman. Mordecai, mounted on a horse and wearing a crown, is led by Haman, who is dressed in the garb of a menial (Pl. xxvii. 2). This miniature bears some resemblance to the corresponding fresco at Dura. How far that resemblance is real rather than accidental must be left for further investigation. This ends the third series.

[1] Margoliouth incorrectly describes the High Priest's headgear as a mitre. He detects a marked resemblance to representations of Christ in this picture of the High Priest. The miniature bears no inscription underneath, the absence of which Margoliouth is inclined to explain as intentional (*Cat. of Heb. MSS.* part iii, p. 425).

[2] The theme of David and Goliath is one of the subjects expressly mentioned by the famous Jewish commentator, Rashī, as having been painted in Talmūdhic times. See supra, p. 59[1].

[3] Fols. 526*b* and 527*a* are blank.

Fourth Series

The fourth and last series, which is inserted at the end of the manuscript, consists of six miniatures. Their style is markedly different from that in the other three series. They show more dramatic force and expression. With one exception, they are all framed in a gilded circle. They are remarkable, too, in other ways. Unlike the majority of the miniatures in the other three series, they follow a rough chronological order. Moreover, five of the six miniatures appear to follow the same sequence as nos. 7–10 in the first series, the exception being no. 4, depicting the budding of Aaron's rod, of which another reproduction is to be found in no. 7 of the third set. This striking resemblance in the sequence of the two sets will help us to explain some of the obscurities in the last set. Another point that is worth noting is that the inscriptions in the fourth set have been added in a later Italian cursive hand.

1. Fol. 740*b*. A picture of a burning city, with a huge reptile at the bottom, depicted with its jaws wide open. The faded inscription below reads: שנ׳ ויצאו וראו בפגרי האנשים, the quotation being part of the last verse of Isaiah (lxvi. 24)—'And they shall go forth and look upon the carcasses of the men.' The writer of the (late) Hebrew inscription appears to have followed Rabbinic exegesis, which reads into the verse a reference to the righteous going forth from Paradise to watch the judgement of the sinners in Hell. (See, for example, the commentaries of Rashī and Ibn Ezra upon this verse, and, more particularly, *Vay-Yikrā Rabbā*, § 32, 1.) On the other hand, it should be remembered that the inscriptions in this series are in a later hand than the rest of the manuscript, and have therefore no special authority. The artist himself may have had the burning of Sodom in mind, a supposition which is strengthened if we take no. 7 in the first set as the corresponding miniature. If this miniature does pictorialize the above verse from Isaiah, it is strange that there is no sign in it of 'the carcasses of the men', a detail which a medieval artist would scarcely have refrained from introducing (Pl. xxviii. 1).

2. Fol. 741*a*. Lot and his two daughters hurrying away from the burning city of Sodom. Lot's wife, lagging behind and looking

82 ILLUMINATED MANUSCRIPTS OF THE WEST

back, is turned into a pillar of salt. The same theme, it will be noted, forms the subject of no. 8 in the first set.

3. Fol. 741*b*. Moses dividing the Red Sea. The author of the Hebrew inscription has strangely missed the point of this miniature. The legend reads: הם ··· ויראו ויקחו איש מטהו ('And they looked and took every man his rod'; Num. xvii. 24 in the Hebrew Bible; xvii. 9 in the R.V.). According to the inscription the miniature should depict the budding of Aaron's rod. That, however, forms the theme of the next miniature. The miniature is quite obviously a representation of Moses smiting the waters of the Red Sea with his rod (some of the waves can actually be seen). The picture thus duplicates the theme of no. 9 in the first set. Moses is here shown, stretching out his rod with one hand and holding the Tables of the Law in the other, thus repeating the same anachronism as we find in the parallel miniature. Behind Moses are to be seen Aaron and five other elders of Israel, viewing the miracle with astonishment (Pl. xxviii. 2).[1]

4. Fol. 742*a*. The budding rod of Aaron. Aaron's rod is shown in the form of a large tree of luxuriant foliage. On either side of it are the barren rods.[2] This miniature breaks the sequence which the other five exhibit. A reproduction of the same theme is to be found in no. 7 of the third series.

5. Fol. 742*b*. The brazen serpent. A very fantastical creature with wings and claws and gilded horn is shown on top, whilst below are seen five Israelites looking up to it. No. 10 (compartment 2) in the first series provides the parallel to this miniature.

6. Fol. 743*a*. Moses striking the rock. He is striking it with some vehemence and anger. Behind him stand two figures, the first being probably Aaron, who points a cautionary finger at his companion. This, the last miniature in the series, is paralleled by no. 10 (compartment 1) in the first series.

[1] Margoliouth (iii. 426), in accepting too readily the Hebrew inscription, gets into difficulties. After quoting the inscription he says: 'The illustration therefore refers to the incident of the budding of Aaron's rod, and the unchanged condition of the other rods. It is, however, difficult to see why only six princes should be present.' The interpretation of the miniature given above disposes of these difficulties.

[2] An attempt may now be made—for the first time—to decipher the 'hardly legible' inscription, as Margoliouth rightly calls it, written below this miniature. It reads: זה מטה אהרן (?) ואחד [ע]שר מטות ('this is the rod of Aaron (?), and the eleven [other] rods').

As has been mentioned before, this manuscript abounds in marginal decorations of animals, grotesques, and other objects, all of them executed with great skill and liveliness. Among these we find a representation of Jonah and the whale, another illustration of Moses dividing the Red Sea (the artist has interpreted his theme very literally and has conscientiously provided us with a red-coloured sea), and another miniature also of the Tree of Life, a theme which so captivated the Jewish imagination.

It has been acutely suggested by Margoliouth that these miniatures were executed by a Christian artist, as he has detected a resemblance to some representations of Christ (unfortunately he does not give examples) in one of the miniatures in our manuscript depicting the High Priest (series 3, no. 14).[1] Our manuscript does reflect very closely the style of illumination current in France at this time.[2] It is also clear that the artist, or rather artists, drew upon the miniatures in vogue at the time in Christian manuscripts. Where Christian illuminated manuscripts represented the scene which the artist was instructed to paint, he would naturally draw upon these sources. On the other hand, where the subject had not been treated in Christian manuscripts he had to fall back upon his own resources or upon the Jewish repertory of picture-sets, if such were available to him. A task for the future will be to determine the relationship of this unique Hebrew manuscript to the Christian and Jewish traditions of illumination.

[1] See *Cat. of Heb. MSS.*, part iii, p. 425, col. 2, note. From the same note it would appear that Margoliouth was also of the opinion that the miniatures were the work of one hand. Judging from the differences of style which the four series exhibit, and from the duplication of themes, it seems probable that several artists were employed.

[2] It has been pointed out to me that many of the miniatures are strongly reminiscent of the representations in stained glass in medieval churches. The Christian affiliations of the manuscript could be profitably studied by a comparison of its miniatures with those of the French Pierpont Morgan manuscript, published for the Roxburghe Club. See *A Book of Old Testament Illustrations*, Cambridge, 1927.

Whether the full-page miniatures were executed by Jewish or Christian artists is a matter upon which one can hardly yet pronounce dogmatically, but it is unlikely that the rest of the marginal decorations in which the manuscript abounds could have been the work of Christian hands. They are so interwoven with the Hebrew text that no artist without a knowledge of Hebrew could have successfully fitted them into the pattern of the page.

The attitude of Rabbinical authority to such illustrated manuscripts is preserved for us in a responsum incorporated in the *Tōsāphōth* (Talmūdhic annotations) of Rabbi Mē'īr ben Baruch of Rothenburg (*c.* 1215–93).[1] The responsum is in answer to a question which had been put to him about the permissibility of pictures (*ṣurōth*) of 'animals and birds' appearing in copies of the *Maḥăzōr* (the service of the Festivals and the Holy Days). While himself deprecating this practice on the ground that 'by gazing upon these pictures people would be diverted from their devotion to their Father in heaven',[2] he nevertheless admits that such practices are not an infraction of the Rabbinical law, whose veto only extended to representational art in the round. This pronouncement is valuable for another reason, as it is, I believe, the earliest extant in the Middle Ages. It is interesting to note that Rabbi Mē'īr was asked only about such illustrations in copies of the *Maḥăzōr*, not of the Hebrew Bible. It is therefore possible that the *Maḥăzōrīm* were the first Hebrew manuscripts to be so illuminated. The question of illustrations of *Biblical* incidents is not raised in this responsum. The date of the British Museum Bible and *Maḥăzōr*, Add. 11639, described above (*circa* 1277–8), coincides with the activities of Rabbi Mē'īr. His attitude to the intrusion of art in religious objects is paralleled by that of Maimonides[3] and—to cite an

[1] The reference is to be found in the *Tōsāphōth* to the tractate Yōmā of the Babylonian Talmūdh, fol. 54*a*, s.v. כרובים דצורתא.

[2] דודאי לא יפה עושים שמסתכלים בצורות הללו אין מכוונין לבם לאביהם שבשמים.

[3] Supra, p. 13.

example from the Fathers of the Church—Clement of Alexandria. Clement, whose interdiction of images is even more comprehensive than that found in the Hebrew Bible, as he includes also painted images, explains the Mosaic prohibition as being 'in order that we might not divert our attention to sensible objects (αἰσθητά), but might proceed to the intelligential (τὰ νοητά)'.[1]

As long as the art of illumination remained the monopoly of the monks in the West, the Jews were unable to illuminate their manuscripts unless they employed Christian artists. By the thirteenth century, however, the practice of illumination and illustration had become partially secularized.[2] Schools arose where the layman could be instructed in these arts. The interest of the Jews in illuminating manuscripts is attested by the survival of a manual of this art compiled by a Jew. This unique manuscript, which forms part of the de Rossi Collection at Parma, was written in Portuguese, but in the Hebrew character, by Abraham ben Judah Ibn Ḥayyīm.[3] Jewish illuminators must have learned their art from Christians in order to produce their illuminated Bibles and prayer-books. The Jews readily acquired these and kindred arts. In fact, they became so adept that by the fifteenth century the Christian Church in Spain found it necessary to ban Jewish artists from working in churches, so keenly was their rivalry felt by their Christian colleagues.[4]

Of the small number of Hebrew Bibles extant Add. 11639 easily takes pride of place by virtue of its age and

[1] *Stromata*, v. 5. 28, 4. See E. Bevan, *Holy Images*, p. 107, from whose translation of Clement I quote.

[2] On the rise of the lay artist in Christian Europe, see, for example, G. G. Coulton, *Art and the Reformation*, Oxford, 1928, chapters ii–v.

[3] See D. Kaufmann, *Die Haggadah von Sarajevo*, p. 299. The date corresponding to A.D. 1262, which is found in the manuscript, and which Kaufmann, following de Rossi, accepted, has been rightly challenged. See the edition of this manual by D. S. Blondheim in *JQR* N.S., xix. 97–135.

[4] See A. L. Mayer in B. Italiener's *Die Darmstädter Pessach-Haggadah*, Leipzig, 1927. Textband, pp. 51–2.

86   ILLUMINATED MANUSCRIPTS OF THE WEST

splendid ornamentation.¹ Of a more modest kind is a Hebrew Bible, or rather portion of a Bible, for it contains only the Pentateuch, the *Haphṭārōth* and the *M'ghillōth*, which was sold on July 20, 1936, at Sotheby's (Lot 25) and is now in Jerusalem, in the Library of Mr. S. Schocken. It is Franco-German in style and, though undated, would appear to belong to the end of the thirteenth or beginning of the fourteenth century. The manuscript has only one page of illustrations, forming the frontispiece. Surrounding the illuminated initial word of the Book of Genesis—בראשית—in the centre of the page, which is enclosed in a frame, are forty-six small medallions illustrating various episodes and subjects recorded in the Pentateuch. Sometimes the illustration overlaps into a second medallion, but, as a rule, one suffices for each subject.

The miniatures are briefly as follows:

(1) Adam and Eve, the serpent, and the tree of knowledge; (2) Adam and Eve chased out of Paradise; (3) Cain slaying Abel; (4) Noah's Ark; (5) Noah planting a vine; (6) The Tower of Babel; (7) Destruction of the Tower; (8) The Sacrifice of Isaac; (9) Isaac blessing Jacob; (10) Esau returning from the chase; (11) Jacob's dream; (12) Jacob wrestling with the angel; (13–14) The (two) dreams of Joseph; (15) Joseph meeting 'a certain man';² (16) Joseph's brethren tending their flocks; (17) Joseph stripped of his coat; (18) Joseph sold to the Ishmaelites; (19) Joseph flees from Potiphar's Wife; (20–1) Joseph interpreting the dreams of Pharaoh's butler and baker; (22) Pharaoh's dream; (23) Joseph interpreting the dream to Pharaoh; (24) The triumph of Joseph; (25–31) Joseph and his brethren in Egypt; (32–3) The bondage of the Israelites in Egypt; (34–5) The discovery of the infant Moses; (36–7) Moses and the burning bush; (38) Moses and Aaron before Pharaoh; (39) The Exodus; (40) Moses dividing the Red Sea; (41) The drowning

¹ Kaufmann mentions with tantalizing brevity a splendid illuminated Hebrew Bible of the Renaissance, in two large octavo volumes, which passed into the possession of the late Baron Edmond de Rothschild in 1877. Its late date, however, would make it more artistically than historically interesting. See *Die Haggadah von Sarajevo*, p. 261.

² The 'certain man' is here drawn as an angel, in conformity with Rabbinic exegesis, which identifies him with the archangel Gabriel.

ILLUMINATED MANUSCRIPTS OF THE WEST 87

of the Egyptians in the Red Sea; (42) Miriam and the women of Israel celebrating the triumph in song and dance; (43) The Revelation of the Law on Mount Sinai; (44) The bunch of grapes from Canaan, borne upon a pole by four men;[1] (45) The Brazen Serpent;[2] and (46) Balaam and his ass (Pl. XXIX).

If we analyse the selection of illustration given in this copy of the Pentateuch, we find that they are all drawn, with the exception of the last four medallions, from Genesis and the first fifteen chapters of Exodus. The later portions of the Pentateuch did not apparently offer the same scope to the artist or make so strong an appeal to him. Furthermore, with the exception of the last four, the illustrations found in this manuscript cover to a large extent, and allowing for individual variations, the same sets of subjects as are contained in copies of the illuminated *Haggādhōth*. Unlike the rather haphazard collection of miniatures in Additional 11639, these illustrations exemplify a coherent and well-defined choice of subjects, and one, moreover, which follows a chronological order.

The remaining extant illustrated Hebrew Bibles, as far as they are known, may be briefly noted. I ought to make it clear that by illuminated Hebrew Bibles I mean such as contain regular picture-sets and not merely isolated miniatures. The sumptuous Hebrew Bible to which Kaufmann makes a short reference still awaits description.[3] Two other illustrated Hebrew Bibles have fortunately been described by Dr. Zofja Ameisenowa. The first of these is a vellum manuscript of German provenance, hailing from Regensburg

---

[1] According to the Biblical account (Num. xiii. 23) the bunch of grapes was carried by two men, not, as here depicted, by four. The first Haggādhāh of Nuremberg has also a medallion of the same subject (fol. 27a), in which two poles are carried crosswise by four men.

[2] The serpent is here represented at the bottom of the medallion, and not, as in the two miniatures in Add. 11639, aloft. An iconographic link is curiously provided by the striking resemblance between the reptile shown here and miniature no. 1, in the fourth series, in Add. 11639. For a description of the latter, see supra, p. 81.

[3] Supra, p. 86[1].

in Bavaria.¹ It is assigned by Dr. Ameisenowa to the fourteenth century. In addition to a patterned *Māsōrāh* and decorated initials it contains six pages of illustrations interspersed through the text. The first of these pages has three miniatures, all of them devoted to the subject of Isaac. They illustrate respectively the circumcision of Isaac, the Sacrifice of Isaac, and the strange story of the Angel of Death bringing the aged Sarah to Mount Moriah to the scene of the Sacrifice.² The Revelation of the Law on Mount Sinai forms the theme of the next miniature. Moses is seen at the top of the mountain, holding one of the Tables of the Law. Midway between the top and the ground below we see Aaron, holding the other Table in one hand and clinging to a tree with the other, as he makes his way down. At the foot of the mountain are Moses and Aaron showing both the Tables of the Law to the elders of Israel. The sacred vessels of the Tabernacle together with a representation of Aaron in his priestly vestments are reproduced in the next miniature. Aaron is shown in the act of lighting the golden Mᵉnōrāh, a full-page reproduction of which appears immediately on the leaf opposite. The pedestal of the Mᵉnōrāh, which is in the form of three lions' claws, is flanked by a lion on each side, thus reproducing a detail which is already noticed in certain specimens of Jewish gold glass found in the catacombs of Rome.

A fifth page of the manuscript is devoted to illustrating the Book of Esther. In the upper compartment we are shown King Ahasuerus extending his sceptre to Esther. A small panel to the left illustrates the hanging of Haman. In the lower compartment, we are shown on the right Mordecai, dressed in regal clothes, stepping upon the prostrate figure of Haman in order to mount his magnificently caparisoned horse. On the left we see the sons of Haman hanging from the gallows. The last of the six pages forms the frontispiece to the Book of Job. The miniature is

---

¹ *Biblja hebrajska xiv-go wieku w Krakowie*, Cracow, 1929.

² Dr. Ameisenowa does not give the source for this form of the legend.

divided into two compartments, the first taking the form of a decorated initial. The lower compartment illustrates Job, in the company of his three friends, sitting on a dunghill and scratching his sores.[1]

A Hebrew Bible, which is now unfortunately lost, but which had been accompanied by a far more extensive repertory of Old Testament illustrations, was the subject of an article by Z. Ameisenowa in the *Monatsschrift für die Geschichte und Wissenschaft des Judentums*.[2] It apparently belonged to the early part of the fifteenth century. Both Gottheil and Dr. Ameisenowa describe it as of Spanish provenance. It was already imperfect when Gottheil saw it, wanting most of *Genesis* and *Chronicles*. According to Gottheil some forty-five illustrations remained, out of an original number which he estimated at sixty. The subjects are as follows:

Exodus. The Entry of the Israelites into Pithom and Rameses; The Ten Plagues; Moses before Pharaoh; The Exodus; The Israelites take with them the bones of Joseph; The Pursuit by Pharaoh; The Crossing of the Red Sea; Miriam's Song; Interior of the Tabernacle, with the lamps and vessels; Aaron before the Altar.

Leviticus. A man kneeling and praying.

Numbers. An Israelite gathering manna.

Deuteronomy. (i) Moses speaks to a group of Israelites. (ii) Joshua receives the wonder-working staff from God.

Judges. An armed knight on horse-back, followed by three men.

1 *Samuel.* Elkanah offers a lamb upon the altar.

1 *Kings.* Bathsheba and the Shunammite woman [Abishag] minister to the sick David.

Isaiah. The prophet speaks to a group of Israelites.

Jeremiah. The prophet preaches to a group of people.

[1] A finely illuminated Hebrew copy of the Hagiographa in the Cambridge University Library (no. 25 in Schiller-Szinessy) has as its sole illustration a representation of Job, his wife, and the Devil. The manuscript is of German origin, and is dated A.D. 1347.

[2] Jahrgang 81 (1937), Breslau, pp. 193–209. This manuscript unfortunately disappeared round about 1935. Dr. Ameisenowa was only able to write about it from photographs. The same manuscript had been previously described by R. Gottheil in *JQR* xvii (1905), pp. 621–5.

Ezekiel. The Vision of the 'Four Living Creatures'.
Hosea. The prophet speaks to women who are sitting on the ground.
Psalms. David playing the harp.
Proverbs. Solomon expounding wisdom.
Job. (1) Satan falling from the skies; (2) Satan before God (?).
Esther. Ahasuerus seated, with a sceptre in his hand.
Lamentations. The Walls of Jerusalem.
Ruth. Ruth, spinning.
Daniel. The prophet seated. In front of him are the golden vessels.
Ezra-Nehemiah. A half-length illustration of the prophet Ezra.
Chronicles. A scribe at work.

We are also indebted to Dr. Ameisenowa for a description of one more illustrated Hebrew Bible.[1] This is a vellum manuscript executed, according to Dr. Ameisenowa, in North-East France about 1300. The illustrations contained in it are taken from a bestiary. It thus shows affinities with the French Bible and *Maḥăzōr* at the British Museum, Additional 11639, which also contains illustrations of fabulous beasts.

In addition to these copies of illustrated Hebrew Bibles, there is one other manuscript which deserves to be recorded. It is not a Hebrew Bible at all, but a translation of the Old Testament into Castilian, provided with copious glosses. It was made by a Spanish Jew of Maqueda and Guadalfajara, Rabbi Moses Arragel by name, and was completed in 1430, the work having been begun in 1422. It was ordered by Don Luis de Guzman, Grand Master of the Order of Calatrava, of Toledo. Apart from its high philological and its literary interest, the manuscript is notable for the inclusion of numerous illustrations, some 334 in all, for the most part inserted in the text, but comprising also six full-page illuminations. A record of the protracted negotiations, as a result of which the natural reluctance and scruples of the Rabbi were finally overcome, is fortunately preserved in the

[1] 'Bestiarius w Biblji Hebrajskiej xiii-go wieku', *Miesięcznik Żydowski*, 1933.

manuscript itself. This Bible, now available to students as a publication of the Roxburghe Club,[1] is one of the treasures of the Duke of Alba's Palace in Madrid. Animated by a fine spirit of tolerance in shining contrast to the spirit of hate and fanaticism that was spreading over the country, Don Luis gave Rabbi Moses Arragel full liberty to express the Jewish standpoint in the manuscript. Moreover, he ordered him to supervise, if not actually to participate in, the execution of the miniatures illustrative of the text. Thanks to the freedom thus extended to him, the volume contains, in addition to the usual illustrations (apparently copied, according to an exchange of correspondence between patron and scribe and translator, from a manuscript in the Cathedral Library of Toledo), a number of miniatures which quite obviously incorporate elements from Rabbinic literature.

One of the most striking of these is the miniature representing the death of Moses (Pl. xxx). This follows entirely the Jewish tradition as it is found, for example, in the Midhrāsh *P^{e}ṭīrath Ahărōn ū-Mōsheh*. In accordance with this account only God is present at the death of the Law-giver, for whom He performs the last rites and ceremonies. One gruesome picture (many of the miniatures exhibit that excessive fondness for the gory so characteristic of the Middle Ages) again lays Rabbinic tradition under tribute. It shows Zimri and the Moabite woman suspended upon the point of Phinehas's lance. According to Jewish legend, Phinehas carried the malefactors out from their tent upon the point of his lance (which incidentally belonged to Moses), in order that all Israel might see that they had been justly punished.[2]

---

[1] *Biblia (Antiguo Testamento). Traducida del hebreo al castellano por Rabi Mosé Arragel de Guadalfajara (1422–1433?) y publicada por el Duque de Berwick y de Alba.* 2 vols., Madrid, 1920, 1922. Art historians will be glad to know that this precious manuscript has escaped the ravages of the Spanish Civil War.

[2] See e.g. L. Ginzberg, *Legends of the Jews*, vol. iii, Philadelphia, 1911, p. 383 sq.

Two more incidents illustrated in this manuscript, both connected with the Book of Esther, derive from Rabbinic lore. The first of these forms the frontispiece to the Book of Esther. The illustration shows Vashti prostrate on the ground, stricken with leprosy. Over her hovers the archangel Gabriel, who, as the Babylonian Talmūdh relates in the tractate M^eghillāh,[1] foiled her in this manner in order that she might be prevented from going to the banquet of Ahasuerus. She is depicted naked, but wearing a crown, for the king had ordered her to appear thus before him and his nobles. The second miniature (Pl. XXXI) which quite unmistakably draws upon the Midhrāsh illustrates the first verse of the sixth chapter of the Book:

'On that night could not the king sleep; and he commanded to bring the book of records of the chronicles, and they were read before the king.'

Rabbinic literature attributes the king's restlessness to the archangel Gabriel, who caused the king to send for the archives and contrived that they should fall open at the place where Mordecai's services to the state were recorded.[2]

The same manuscript contains several other illustrations which reveal how deeply permeated it is by Jewish thought and tradition. There are several representations of the Mercy Seat, as well as full-page miniatures of the golden M^enōrāh, the service of the Temple, and Moses bringing down the Tables of the Law from Mount Sinai. In this last illustration the opening words of each of the Ten Commandments are given in Hebrew. Judging from the style of the writing this could scarcely have been executed by a non-Jew.

The striking resemblance between a section of the Ezekiel panel on the walls of the synagogue at Dura-Europos with a miniature illustrating the same theme in the Alba Bible has already been noticed. That this resemblance

[1] 12b.
[2] This incident is also found depicted in copies of the illuminated M^eghillāh. See D. Kaufmann, *Die Haggadah von Sarajevo*, p. 264.

ILLUMINATED MANUSCRIPTS OF THE WEST

should persist in spite of the lapse of twelve hundred years which separates the two paintings, is indeed remarkable. But the student of iconography is often impressed by the way in which the same artistic conventions and motifs are perpetuated through the ages. The instinct for conservatism is as strong in the artist as in other members of society. The average craftsman is usually content to concentrate upon the quality of his workmanship rather than trouble himself about originality of design.

The number of extant illustrated Hebrew Bibles, of which descriptions have been published, is small indeed. The many Biblical codices which are distinguished by occasional marginal illustrations or by isolated miniatures cannot here be considered. With the exception of the Pentateuch (if the Pentateuch may be considered as a single book) and Esther, single books of the Hebrew Bible are not often found illustrated. In contrast to the Christian Psalters many of which are often so lavishly illustrated an histcriated Hebrew copy of the Psalms is exceptional. A rare example of such a work is to be found in the de Rossi collection at Parma (No. 510).[1] This manuscript which contains the text, accompanied by the commentary of Abraham Ibn Ezra, is embellished with ornamentation, which often takes the form of illustrating the contents of the accompanying psalms. There are, for example, miniatures illustrating David playing the harp, Saul in flight, and the weeping exiles in Babylon referred to in Psalm 137, who hung up their harps in despair when they recalled the glories of the past. A part of the Hebrew Bible which is often illustrated is the Book of Esther. An adequate consideration of such illustrated copies of the *M^eghillāh* would require a chapter by itself. But as the fashion of illustrating them does not seem to have developed to any extent until post-medieval times, we have excluded them from our survey.[2] For similar reasons a consideration of the

[1] D. Kaufmann, in *Die Haggadah von Sarajevo*, p. 262.
[2] See D. Kaufmann, op. cit., pp. 262–7, for a brief survey of the

illuminated *Kᵉthubbōth* (marriage certificates) has been omitted.

The early illuminated Hebrew prayer-books, both *Siddūrīm* and *Maḥăzōrīm*, generally confine themselves to non-representational art, the ornamentation taking the form of illuminated initials, grotesques, and flower-and-leaf patterns. They include occasionally Biblical illustrations, but not as part of a regular picture-sequence. An early Franco-German *Maḥăzōr* at the British Museum, Additional 22413, provides an interesting example of such occasional illustration. While not actually dated, it may be assigned on palaeographical grounds and from the evidence of the style of illumination, to the latter part of the thirteenth century. The manuscript is a fragment only, containing the service of *Shābhū'ōth* (Pentecost) and *Sukkōth* (Feast of Tabernacles). It has a number of miniatures, but only two are definitely illustrative. The first represents Moses receiving the Tables of the Law on Mount Sinai. As the Festival of *Shābhū'ōth* celebrates the Revelation of the Law, such a miniature calls for no comment. The second illustrative miniature is the headpiece to the Book of Ruth, which is read on the same festival. It depicts a harvest scene, with Ruth amongst the reapers.[1] A curious feature of both these

subject. The hanging of Haman and his sons, and the elevation of Mordecai are two of the most popular themes depicted. Copies of the Book of Esther are always written in scroll form. It is thus the only book of the Hebrew Bible in which the old tradition is strictly adhered to, whether the copy was intended for private or public use.

[1] The rarity of illustrations to the Book of Ruth in Hebrew manuscripts may possibly be connected with a similar scarcity of such miniatures in Christian manuscripts. M. R. James, in describing a miniature of Ruth gleaning in the famous twelfth-century Latin Bible at Lambeth Palace, remarks upon the uncommonness of such illustrations. See his *Descriptive Catalogue of the Manuscripts in the Library of Lambeth Palace*, pt. 1, Cambridge, 1930, no. 3, p. 6. Another miniature of the same theme is to be found in the Latin Bible at the B. M., Royal 1. E. ix, f. 62b. It is interesting to note that the Castilian version of the Hebrew Bible by Moses Arragel, whose picture-sets betray Jewish as well as Christian influences, contains miniatures illustrating

ILLUMINATED MANUSCRIPTS OF THE WEST 95

miniatures, which is found also in other Hebrew manuscripts, is that several of the human figures are drawn with grotesque heads of animals.

In some manuscripts the descriptive interest of the miniatures is found to be secondary to their expository function, the intention being not so much to tell a story as to point a moral. A late Italian *Maḥăzōr* preserved in the Jewish Theological Seminary of America, New York, contains a number of interesting illustrations drawn from the Hebrew Bible. Amongst them are pictures illustrating the Aramaic *piyyūṭīm* on the Ten Commandments recited on the Festival of *Shābhū'ōth*. The Sacrifice of Isaac, for example, accompanies the exposition of the Fifth Commandment, the willingness of Isaac being considered a supreme example of filial obedience. Similarly, a picture of Joseph and Potiphar's wife illustrates the *piyyūṭ* upon the commandment against adultery. A representation of Adam and Eve and the Serpent does duty for the Tenth Commandment (against covetousness). These illustrations thus partake of the character of the *Bibles moralisées* of the Middle Ages.[1] They are introduced to drive home the moral implicit in the Biblical text. The inclusion of certain Biblical illustrations is also to be noted in many of the classic works of Rabbinic literature. A beautifully illuminated copy in the British Museum of the *Arbā'āh Ṭūrīm*, the code of Jacob ben Asher, written in 1473–5, probably in Italy, has a miniature of Adam and Eve.[2] A manuscript in the de Rossi collection, no. 878, containing the biblical commentaries of Rashī and Abraham Ibn Ezra includes, amongst the Book of Ruth. For a miniature of Ruth in a Hebrew Bible, see supra, p. 90.

[1] The British Museum MS. of Somme le Roi, Add. 28162, provides yet another link with this kind of illustration. This copy, whose date is about 1300, contains, amongst other things, miniatures illustrating the Decalogue. See J. A. Herbert, *Illuminated Manuscripts*, London, 1911, pp. 201–2.

[2] Harl. 5716–17. The miniature is to be found in vol. 2, fol. 6b.

many ornamentations and miniatures, an illustration of Moses expounding the Law to the Israelites. More curious examples of Old Testament illustration are to be found in several copies of Rashī's commentary, which show a map of Canaan, in addition to representations of the Tabernacle and its sacred vessels.[1]

More than any other book it is the *Haggādhāh*, the ritual of the Eve of Passover in the home, which came to be associated *par excellence* with Biblical illustrations, although itself not forming part of the Hebrew Bible. In this respect the *Haggādhāh* occupies an analogous position to the profusely illustrated copies of the Book of Hours in the Christian Church. Copies of such illuminated *Haggādhōth* have survived in quite large numbers. They may be roughly divided into two classes, according as they are distinguished by regular picture-sets or only by occasional and sporadic illustrations. The latter kind need not detain us, as the range of their Biblical illustrations is small and their subjects usually included in those other *Haggādhōth*, which are accompanied by definite picture-cycles. The manuscripts of the first class exhibit certain common features. The miniatures are to be found assembled either at the beginning or end of the codex, although sometimes they occur elsewhere in the book. The range and choice of illustrations are usually restricted. They may start from the Creation and proceed to the celebration of the first Passover, thus illustrating pictorially the salient episodes comprised in the Book of Genesis and the first fifteen chapters of Exodus. We may observe that the same subjects, with little variation, are chosen in almost all the manuscripts. Sometimes the range is restricted to the Book of Exodus, beginning with the events recorded in the first chapter, and continuing to the celebration of the first Passover. Such a selection seems more in harmony with the contents of the *Haggādhāh*, which deals primarily with the Exodus. At other times, again, the picture-sets begin

[1] See Kaufmann, op. cit., pp. 288–9.

ILLUMINATED MANUSCRIPTS OF THE WEST 97

with the first chapter of the Book of Exodus and continue the story to the celebration of the First Passover, but incorporate at the end illustrations of the salient events recorded in the Book of Genesis and other portions of the Hebrew Bible. The Spanish *Haggādhāh* at the British Museum, Oriental 2737, it is interesting to note, begins with a pictorial illustration of the events recorded in the first five chapters of Exodus. But the four concluding miniatures are devoted to a representation of the Sacrifice of Isaac.[1] While illuminated *Haggādhōth* generally confine their illustrations to the above-mentioned portions of the Pentateuch, we occasionally meet in them with representations of subsequent events in Biblical history.

The Second *Haggādhāh* at Nuremberg,[2] for example, shows us, in addition to the usual pictures illustrating Genesis and Exodus i–xv, Moses receiving the Law on Mount Sinai, and Joshua and the Angel, these two themes following each other upon two successive pages of the manuscript;[3] the parents of the infant Samuel presenting him to Eli; Samson rending the lion, and bringing down the palace of the Philistines; David and Goliath, the Judgement of Solomon, Jonah and the whale; and, lastly, a picture so often met with in both manuscript and printed copies of the *Haggādhāh*, the prophet Elijah riding on an ass and proclaiming upon his horn the coming of the Messiah. Another copy of the *Haggādhāh* included in a fifteenth-century manuscript which contains also the Psalms, Job, Proverbs, and the Daily Prayers, and which is (or was) in the possession of the Rothschild family in Paris, includes a number of interesting

---

[1] An odd blank leaf in the middle of the volume (fol. 35*b*) was utilized by the artist for a representation of Samson slaying the lion. For a description of the manuscript see *Catalogue of the Hebrew and Samaritan Manuscripts in the British Museum*, part ii, p. 203, No. 609.

[2] The miniatures, which do not always follow a regular sequence, are carefully described in *Die Haggadah von Sarajevo*, pp. 125–70.

[3] The juxtaposition of Moses and the Law, and Joshua and the Angel supports the interpretation of two of the portrait panels in the frescoes at Dura as representations of the same theme. See supra, p. 34.

O

illustrations supplementing the usual selection. Among them are Sisera pursued by the archers, Daniel in the lions' den, and two pictures illustrating the story of Esther, one depicting her assembling her compatriots and proclaiming a three-day fast, the other showing Haman hanging from a tree. The presence of these two pictures in the text of the *Haggādhāh* may evoke surprise until we remember that Rabbinic tradition associates both these events with the time of the Passover.[1] The miniatures to the Books of the Psalms, Job, and Proverbs in this manuscript respectively illustrate David with his harp, Job restored to prosperity, in the midst of his family, and Solomon on his throne. Illustrations of Biblical interest in the part containing the Daily Prayers are the Passage of the Red Sea, and the hanging of the ten sons of Haman.

The illustrated *Haggādhōth* have been more fortunate than the Hebrew Bibles in attracting the interest of scholars. As long ago as 1898 a facsimile reproduction of the famous *Haggādhāh* of Sarajevo appeared in Vienna. Three famous scholars, Julius von Schlosser, David Kaufmann, and David Heinrich Müller collaborated in its production. Unfortunately, the pioneering work of these scholars did not stimulate others to further research upon the fascinating problems connected with the iconography of the Passover *Haggādhāh*. One can imagine what a brilliant piece of constructive scholarship David Kaufmann might have built up had he lived to witness the latest discoveries brought to light by the excavations of the ancient synagogues of the East. The time, however, was not ripe to bring this subject into focus with the *Bildstoff* of Christian iconography.

The picture-sets found in the *Haggādhāh* at Sarajevo follow a well-defined sequence, which recurs regularly in this type of illustrated Spanish *Haggādhōth*. A résumé of Biblical history from the Creation down to the wanderings of the Israelites in the wilderness is pictorially illustrated by a selection of the most memorable incidents recorded in

[1] *Die Haggadah von Sarajevo*, p. 207.

ILLUMINATED MANUSCRIPTS OF THE WEST

the Pentateuch. Two of these pictures may be singled out for special comment. One of them depicts the oasis of Elim, showing affinities with a similar theme in the frescoes of Dura, about which I have already spoken. The other exemplifies similar affinities. It is a representation of the Temple as it will appear when rebuilt, a picture, which I venture to think explains the *raison d'être* of a similar subject depicted at Dura, whose meaning has hitherto puzzled scholars.

Another characteristic illustrated *Haggādhāh* of the Spanish rite, not so well known as the Sarajevo MS., is the British Museum MS. Additional 27210. From the style of its illumination, which is French in character, it may be assigned to the late thirteenth century. The first fourteen folios, of which only one side is used, are devoted to miniatures illustrating the most salient events of Biblical history from the Creation to the time of the first celebration of the Passover. Each page is divided into four compartments, to which descriptions (in Hebrew) are attached.

The following is a description of the fourteen pages of miniatures.[1] They are all executed in colours upon a gold ground. One side of the leaf has been used for the painting of the miniatures, a later scribe having filled in the blank pages with ritual matter relating to the Passover.

Fol. 2b. *Compartment* 1. Adam names the animals. 2. Eve emerges from the rib of Adam (r.).[2] Adam and Eve and the Serpent, the latter twined round the Tree of Knowledge and facing Eve (l.). An angel in the sky points an admonitory finger at them. 3. Cain and Abel bring their offerings (r.). The slaying of Abel (l.). An angel in the sky points to the scene of the murder. 4. Noah, his wife and children behind him, helps the animals out of the Ark. Amongst the animals shown is a pig![3]

---

[1] The miniatures, which are to be read from right to left (like the Hebrew alphabet), have not been previously described in detail. For a description of the manuscript see G. Margoliouth, op. cit., ii, pp. 200–2.

[2] The abbreviations r., l., and c. denote *right*, *left*, and *centre* respectively.

[3] Possibly an indication that the artist was a Christian. That is not

Fol. 3a. 1. Noah plants a vine (r.). Noah carried out drunk by his sons (l.). 2. The Tower of Babel. 3. Nimrod, seated upon a throne, orders Abraham to be cast into the fiery furnace. (This incident does not, of course, figure in the Hebrew Bible, but is drawn from the Midhrāsh.) Abraham is seen falling into the arms of a bearded angel, who is no doubt intended to represent God himself.[1] 4. Abraham and the Three Angels.

to say that representations of swine are excluded by Jewish illuminators. Both the so-called First and Second *Haggādhōth* of Nuremberg contain illustrations of this animal. In both these cases, however, there seems to have been a cogent reason for its introduction. In the First *Haggādhāh* a boar chase is depicted, in the Second a hog is introduced in order to illustrate the effects of drunkenness. For reproductions of these two miniatures, see *Die Haggadah von Sarajevo*, plates xi and xix. A picture of the animal in an incongruous setting is provided by a Christian illuminator in the famous Latin twelfth-century illuminated Bible at Lambeth Palace, where the frontispiece to Leviticus portrays 'what looks like a pig' being killed by two men. See M. R. James and C. Jenkins, *A Descriptive Catalogue of the Manuscripts in the Library of Lambeth Palace*, pt. 1, Cambridge, 1930, no. 3, p. 6.

A miniature betraying strong Christian influences is that found on fol. 10b, compartment 2, which represents Aaron meeting Moses and his wife and children on their way back to Egypt from Midian. This bears a marked likeness to the more or less stereotyped representations of the 'Flight of the Holy Family into Egypt'. A rare example of a Hebrew Bible illuminated by a Christian artist is to be found in the Laurentian Library of Florence. See Kaufmann, op. cit., p. 302. An illustrated *Haggādhāh*, once forming part of the collection of Mr. Elkan N. Adler and now in the Library of the Jewish Theological Seminary of New York, contains illustrations attributed on the authority of Fairfax Murray and Olschki to Bonifacio il Giovine Veneziano. See B. Italiener, *die Darmstädter Pessach-Haggadah*, Textband, p. 290, no. 75. For a convincing refutation of the claims made on behalf of a Hebrew manuscript, containing a ritual compilation, that it was illuminated by Giotto, see E. Panofsky, 'Giotto and Maimonides in Avignon', *Journal of the Walters Art Gallery*, vol. iv, 1941, pp. 26–44. Further examples of the 'Christianization' of Jewish art are given, loc. cit., p. 35 and p. 43, note 18. I am indebted to Dr. Otto Kurz for this reference. He also points out to me that Panofsky has overlooked a previous article upon this manuscript by E. N. Adler, who was inclined to accept the attribution. See 'A Hebrew MS. illustrated by Giotto', *J.Q.R.* xi (1899), pp. 679–82.

[1] According to Rabbinic accounts it was God himself who went

Abraham in response to the angels' question points in the direction of Sarah.

Fol. 4*b*. 1. Lot and his daughter escape from the burning city (r.). Lot's wife transformed into a pillar of salt (c.). The destruction of Sodom (l.). 2. The Sacrifice of Isaac. The two servants with the ass, the latter only partially shown (r.). The ram caught by its horns in the bush (c.). An angel appears in the sky. Abraham, about to slay Isaac is restrained by the angel, who calls to him (l.). 3. Isaac blesses Jacob. Isaac, blind, feels Jacob, behind whom stands Rebecca. Esau returns from the chase (r.). 4. Jacob's Dream. Angels ascending and descending the ladder.

Fol. 5*a*. 1. Jacob wrestles with the angel (r.). Crossing the Jabbok (l.). 2. Joseph's Dreams. 3. Joseph's Brethren (r.). Jacob rebukes Joseph (l.). 4. Joseph meets an angel (r.). (According to the account in Genesis xxxvii. 15, he met 'a certain man' when he went in search of his brothers. It is the Midhrāsh which exalts this mysterious person into the archangel Gabriel.) The brothers of Joseph plotting to kill him as they see him coming (l.).

Fol. 6*b*. 1. Joseph is stripped of his coat and cast into a well. His coat is dipped in the blood of a slaughtered goat. 2. He is sold to the Ishmaelites. 3. Joseph's brethren bring the blood-stained coat to Jacob their father (r.). Jacob rends his clothes in grief (l.). 4. In two (horizontal) sections. (i) Potiphar's wife catches hold of Joseph's cloak as he flees from her. (ii) Joseph interprets the dreams of Pharaoh's butler and baker.

down into the fiery furnace in order to save Abraham. Strange as it may seem, representations of God are not wholly excluded from Hebrew illuminated manuscripts. In the famous Sarajevo *Haggādhāh* he is depicted in the form of a young and beardless man, resting from his labours on the Sabbath. The representation of the Deity as an old man, as in the manuscript described above, recalls similar miniatures in the Christian medieval manuscripts. On the other hand, the depiction of God as a young and beardless man, as in the Sarajevo *Haggādhāh*, relates him to one of the miniatures in the considerably earlier Cotton Genesis, a manuscript which has been assigned to the sixth century or even earlier. According to the coloured copy of this miniature, made for Peiresc—the original is hopelessly damaged—God is there depicted as young and beardless (thus resembling the portraits of Christ in the first period of Christian art), with fair hair and a cruciform nimbus. We know that Augustine condemned as impious any attempt to represent God pictorially (*De Fide et Symbolo*, ch. vii). Contemporary Rabbinic

102   ILLUMINATED MANUSCRIPTS OF THE WEST

Fol. 7a. 1. Pharaoh's Dreams. 2. Joseph interprets the dreams. Pharaoh's magicians are baffled (r.). Joseph interprets the dream to Pharaoh (l.).[1] 3. Joseph and his Brethren. Joseph speaks harshly to his brethren and orders Simeon to be bound in their presence. 4. Joseph embraces young Benjamin, while his brothers look on in astonishment.

Fol. 8b. 1. Jacob blesses Pharaoh. 2. Jacob on his sick-bed crosses his hands in blessing Ephraim and Manasseh. 3. The Death of Jacob. The bier containing his body is surrounded by his mourning children (r.). Pharaoh, surrounded by his courtiers, raises his hands in grief (l.). 4. The Pharaoh, 'who knew not Joseph', upraiding the two Jewish midwives for sparing the newly born male children of the Israelites. In front is seen the Nile into which the children are being thrown.[2]

Fol. 9a. 1. The discovery of the infant Moses. The princess who is bathing with her two maids in the Nile comes upon the ark containing the infant Moses. From a point of vantage on the banks of the river the sister of Moses watches them. 2. The princess, accompanied by her two maids, presents the infant to Pharaoh and his court. 3. The Egyptian smiting the Israelite (r.). Moses kills the Egyptian (l.). 4. Moses rescues the daughters of Reuel from the shepherds (Pl. XXXI. 1).

Fol. 10b. 1. Moses and the Burning Bush. 2. Moses and his

authority would no doubt have been equally outraged by such a practice. In connexion with representations of God found in the medieval illuminated manuscripts of the *Haggādhāh* it is well to remember that the service of the *Haggādhāh* was primarily for the home, not (as a general rule) for the synagogue. Copies of it could therefore be regarded as falling outside the orbit of Rabbinical jurisdiction, or, at least, as not subject to the same degree of rigour. For a representation of the Deity found upon a Jewish tombstone, see supra, p. 11[1]. For similar representations in primitive Christian art, see Dom. H. Leclercq, in *Dictionnaire de l'Archéologie Chrétienne*, s.v. 'Dieu'. For a discussion of the early Christian attitude to such illustrations, see E. Bevan, *Holy Images*, pp. 119, 159–61.

[1] The Hebrew caption is wrong. According to it the miniature illustrates the shaving of Joseph and the changing of his clothes. It is clear, however, that what this section of the miniature represents is Joseph interpreting the dream to Pharaoh.

[2] The miniatures depicting Pharaoh upraiding the Jewish midwives, and the discovery of the infant Moses, show some affinities with the sections illustrating the same themes in the wall-paintings at Dura.

ILLUMINATED MANUSCRIPTS OF THE WEST 103

family returning to Egypt.[1] He is met by Aaron on the way. 3. Moses and Aaron performing miracles before the worshipping Israelites. 4. Moses and Aaron in the presence of Pharaoh and his wise men (Pl. XXXI. 2).

Fol. 11a. 1. The Bondage of the Israelites. An Egyptian overseer mounted on a kind of rostrum directs the work of the Israelites (r.). One, on the right, carries a load of straw. Another treads the clay (c.). Israelites, including a woman with a child, preparing the bricks (l.). 2. Building the store cities. 3. Moses and Aaron performing miracles in the presence of Pharaoh. The Rod of Aaron changed into a serpent devours the similarly changed rods of Pharaoh's magicians. 4. The Plagues of Egypt. The First Plague. The Waters of the Nile are turned into blood. Moses and Aaron, the latter with his rod (r.). Pharaoh, seated (l.). The River Nile turned to red, with three blue fishes rising to the surface (c.). On the other side of the Nile are two Egyptians digging for pure water.

Fol. 12b. 1. The Second Plague. Frogs. Aaron (?) stirs the waters of the Nile with his rod (r.).[2] The frogs swarm into the kitchen utensils (c.). Pharaoh is shown seated (r.). 2. The Third Plague. Lice. Moses and Aaron are immune, whilst Pharaoh and his household, as well as the animals, are all depicted as suffering grievously from the effects of the plague. 3. The Fourth Plague. The plague here shown is that of wild animals, not of insects, thus following the Rabbinic interpretation. 4. The Fifth Plague. The Murrain.

Fol. 13a. 1. The Sixth Plague. Boils. Moses and Aaron casting ashes from a bowl up in the air (r.). Pharaoh, attended by a physician (l.). At his feet sit two magicians. 2. The Seventh Plague. Hail. Moses stretches out his hands towards heaven (r.). Hail falls on a tree, under which a shepherd and his flock have taken refuge (c.). Pharaoh, seated, his left hand being raised (l.). 3. The Eighth Plague. Locusts. Moses and Aaron, the latter with his rod (r.). In the centre and to the left are two trees, their branches swarming with locusts. 4. The Ninth Plague. Darkness. The miniature is divided into two horizontal sections. (i) The Egyptians, including the King, groping in the dark-

[1] As mentioned above (supra, p. 99[3]), this miniature is strikingly similar to representations of the 'Flight of the Holy Family into Egypt' in Christian manuscripts and paintings.

[2] The caption describes him as Moses, but according to the Biblical account (Exod. viii. 5) it is Aaron who is told to stretch his rod over the rivers and cause frogs to come up over the land.

ness. (ii) The Israelites, immune to the plague, helping themselves to the possessions of the Egyptians.[1]

Fol. 14b. 1. The Death of the First-Born. In two sections. (i) The Angel of Death smites the First-Born (r.). The death of Pharaoh's first-born (l.). He is held in his nurse's arms, while the queen joins her in lamentation. (ii) The funeral of the King's first-born. Women in black precede the bier, which is borne upon poles by six members of the bereaved family. 2. Pharaoh standing with his courtiers on the steps of his palace, watches the Israelites depart. The latter are seen raising their right hand high above them, and holding the unleavened dough in their left. 3. Pharaoh and his warriors in hot pursuit. 4. Moses and the Israelites pass through the divided waters of the Red Sea, whilst Pharaoh and his host are engulfed in the waves (Pl. xxxii. 1).

Fol. 15a. 1. Miriam, the sister of Aaron and Moses, celebrates, in the company of the women of Israel, the defeat of Pharaoh, with music and dance. This charming miniature illustrates incidentally the love of music so deeply ingrained in the Jewish people. 2–4. The preparation of the Passover (Pl. xxxii. 2).

The manuscript is typical of the majority of illustrated *Haggādhōth* in the selection of its themes, if not in their individual treatment. One of the subjects which awaits consideration is the exact relationship of the picture-cycles preserved in the *Haggādhōth* to the mural paintings of Dura and the mosaics of the early Palestinian synagogues on the one hand and Christian iconography on the other. The subject is still in its embryonic stage, but even a cursory examination of these *Haggādhōth* recalls to us their striking analogies with the early Jewish picture-sets discovered at Dura-Europos.

It is necessary to deal, however briefly, with the other category of Hebrew illuminated Bibles, I mean the non-representational kind. These do not include picture-sets depicting Old Testament subjects, but confine themselves to representations of inanimate objects mentioned in the

[1] It is Rabbinic exegesis which associates the spoiling of the Egyptians with the plague of darkness, in contrast to the account in Exodus, where the Israelites are bidden to borrow objects from the Egyptians apparently after this plague had come to an end (Exod. xi. 2–3).

Hebrew Bible, like the Golden Menōrāh and the sacred vessels of the Tabernacle, to arabesques, patterns of flower and leaf, to animals and grotesques. There is, however, no rigid line of demarcation between the representational and the non-representational kind of illuminated Hebrew Bibles. Occasionally a picture will insinuate itself upon the margin depicting a figure or episode out of the Hebrew Bible. Sometimes frontispieces will contain a decorative rather than descriptive treatment of a biblical theme. Broadly speaking, the two classes of illuminated manuscripts can be readily distinguished. The non-representational class far outnumbers the representational, copies of which are, indeed, rare, as I have already mentioned.

These non-representational illuminated Hebrew Bibles exhibit certain common features, whether their provenance be Spain, Portugal, France, Germany, or Italy. They almost invariably devote one or more pages to illustrating the Golden Menōrāh and other sacred vessels of the Tabernacle. Sometimes one, occasionally both, the Songs of Moses (Exod. xv; Deut. xxxii) have painted borders, a feature which it shares with the considerably earlier Hebrew Bibles of the East and which, in the case of the First Song, is reproduced in some of the earliest printed Hebrew Bibles. The beginning of the pericopes is as a rule distinguished by ornamentation. The initials of the various books forming the Hebrew Bible are similarly the object of decorative treatment. Sometimes the special Masoretic lists preceding or coming at the end of the manuscript are enclosed in richly illuminated borders. The *Māsōrāh*, the textual apparatus of the Hebrew Bible, became early the subject of artistic experimentation. Instead of soberly accompanying the text on the margins, it began to assume fantastic shapes. This practice became so common that the Rabbis found it necessary to curb the exuberance of scribes and artists. We find, for example, Rabbi Judah ben Samuel he-Ḥāsīdh in his *Sēpher Ḥăsīdhīm* expressly forbidding the arrangement of the *Māsōrāh* in the form of animals, birds and the like.¹ The warning appears to have had little effect in checking this growing fashion. One interesting conclusion is revealed by this usage. This treatment of the *Māsōrāh* demonstrates clearly that its presence in the Hebrew Bible had come to be considered in the light of an ornamental appendage. It had crystallized into an artistic convention, having largely ceased to become the object of serious study.

Another artistic convention is found to develop in the fourteenth and fifteenth centuries. This consisted in the inclusion of some extraneous work or treatise to go with the Hebrew Bible, which in some way or other was related to the sacred text. This feature is particularly noticeable in Spanish and Portuguese manuscripts of the Old Testament. Such an extra-Biblical treatise would be incorporated at the beginning of the manuscript or would be divided into two halves, for the beginning and end of the manuscript respectively. The work might consist of the list of the 613 positive and negative commandments of the Law, the *Mikhlōl* of David Ḳimḥī, containing his Biblical dictionary, or some similar work. It was upon these non-Biblical treatises that the artist would lavish all the resources of his skill and experience. Such texts provided a kind of safety valve to the artist for the free and untrammelled exercise of his imagination, in contrast to the Scriptures themselves, where he would refrain from a sense of religious scruple from overloading the page with too much ornament. The finest examples of illuminated Hebrew Bibles of the non-representational kind are to be found in the manuscripts of Spanish and Portuguese origin. It is in them that the skill of the Jewish artist is best exemplified. The more sober and restrained artistic traditions of Moorish Spain are reflected in these Biblical manuscripts to a greater degree than the exuberant Gothic fashions of the northern countries. The Moorish style, modified and adapted to the Hebrew manuscript, suited the Jewish artistic genius admirably. Moreover, the grave and monumental beauty of the square

¹ *Die Haggadah von Sarajevo*, p. 257.

Hebrew Sephardi script harmonized with singular felicity with this style of illumination, the two blending with extraordinary effectiveness. In this script the Jewish calligrapher found to hand an instrument of incomparable dignity, whose calligraphic possibilities could be fully exploited.

A good example of the representation of the Golden Menōrāh and the other sacred vessels is provided by Codex no. 7, a Hebrew Bible copied by Solomon ben Raphael in the Ghetto of Perpignan in the year 1299.[1] The Golden Menōrāh occupies more than half of the right compartment. Round its base are distributed the tongs (מלקחים) and the fire-pans (מחתות), two of each being shown. The stone steps leading up to the altar are also depicted, one on each side of the base of the Menōrāh. The lower compartment contains in the centre the pot of manna and, to the right and left of it, the budding rod of Aaron and the barren rods belonging to the other eleven tribes, only one of the latter being shown. On the left we have a picture of the Cherubim over the Mercy Seat and, below it, the two Tables of the Law. Beneath are seen two of the pans used for holding the frankincense, which, according to the Talmūdh, belonged to the Table of the Shewbread. This object is shown immediately below, with the six loaves arranged in tiers on each side of it. If we compare the list of objects with the analogous sets found in the mural painting at Dura or the mosaic floor of Bēth-Alphā, we are struck by the disappearance of the *lūlābh* and the *ethrōgh*, the palm-branch and citron, whose representation is such a familiar feature in the coins, gold glass, and other early remains of Jewish archaeology.

An illuminated Hebrew Pentateuch once belonging to the Duke of Sussex and acquired by the British Museum after his death shows some interesting and unusual features. The manuscript was executed, probably in the late thirteenth or early part of the fourteenth century, in the Franco-German style.[2] Besides the Pentateuch, which is accom-

[1] In the Bibliothèque Nationale.   [2] Add. 15282.

panied by the Targūm (the Aramaic version), it contains the five *Mʿghillōth* and the *Haphṭārōth*. Each of the five books of the Tōrāh has a frontispiece executed in gold and colours, with the first word in large gold letters in the centre of the page. The frontispiece to the Book of Numbers [1] (Pl. xxxiii) is interesting as embodying descriptive pictorial elements in its decorative scheme. The subject, four armed warriors carrying banners, is drawn from the opening chapters of the Book. The treatment of the picture, however, emphasizes the decorative aspects rather than the descriptive. It is not a picture which tells a story primarily, but employs motifs drawn from the Biblical narrative decoratively.

Initials in large gold letters enclosed in ornamental borders also distinguish four of the *Mʿghillōth* and the *Haphṭārōth*. The Book of Lamentations, for obvious reasons, has no ornamentation, its mournful contents being scarcely considered suitable for illumination. In this connexion it is interesting to note that some illuminated Hebrew Bibles, like the famous G. 1 at Trinity College, Cambridge, for example, handle the problem of suitable illumination for the Book of Lamentations in a different way. Instead of dispensing with decoration entirely, they content themselves with painting the borders in dark and subdued colours. There seems, however, to have been no hard and fast rule in dealing with such a problem.[2]

[1] Id., fol. 179*b*.
[2] One manuscript of Biblical contents at the British Museum, Add. 9405 (its date corresponds to 1309), has, appropriately enough, a representation of two mourning figures at the beginning of Lamentations. See Margoliouth, op. cit., i, no. 143, p. 107. Other manuscripts, again, make no distinction in the ornamentation of this Book. The de Castro Pentateuch in the collection of Mr. D. S. Sassoon, written in a German hand in 1344, illustrates the beginning of Lamentations with the figure of the *Ḥazzān* (reader) wearing a *Ṭallīth* (praying-shawl) with his hand over his face, as a sign of grief. The illuminated initial is painted 'in red and blue, with raised silver buttons, in a many-coloured frame'. See D. S. Sassoon, *Descriptive Catalogue*, vol. i, London, 1932, pp. 19–21 (no. 506).

ILLUMINATED MANUSCRIPTS OF THE WEST

The same illuminated Pentateuch (Add. 15282) furnishes also a good example of the figured *Māsōrāh*. The margins, more particularly in the early part of the book, abound in all kinds of pen-and-ink drawings, made up of the Masoretic notes. They range from geometrical patterns to representations of flowers, trees, animals, and other objects. The patterns and figures are not infrequently connected with the subject-matter of the Biblical text.

For example, a very ingeniously executed representation of the ram, caught by its horns in a tree, accompanies the narrative of the Sacrifice of Isaac.[1] A drawing of Jacob's Ladder, similarly constructed out of the Masoretic text, is to be found in the margin on the same page where this incident is related in the Book of Genesis.[2] This connexion between the figured *Māsōrāh* and the Biblical subject-matter has been pointed out in the case of another manuscript at the British Museum by Margoliouth.[3] It shows the calligrapher, like the miniaturist—they may have been in this case one and the same person—utilizing Biblical themes both decoratively and descriptively.

At the expense of extending this lecture beyond the hallowed limits of sixty minutes, I feel that I should do less than justice to my subject if I refrained from describing, however summarily, some of the finest and most characteristic Sephardi illuminated Hebrew Bibles of the non-representational kind known to me.

Fortunately, we have in England three such specimens, all of them superb, of the calligrapher's and illuminator's art. One is in private possession, another in the British Museum, and the third at the Bodleian.

The first of these Bibles, the Famous Farchi Bible, so called because it belonged to that family for many years, is

[1] Id., fol. 28*a*, in illustration of Gen. xxi.   [2] Id., fol. 39*a* (Gen. xxvii).

[3] Add. 21160. See Margoliouth, op. cit., part i, p. 50, col. 1. This manuscript contains designs constructed out of Masoretic notes representing Jonah and the whale, and Jonah and the gourd. The same manuscript contains a similarly constructed 'Tree of Jesse'.

the earliest, the date of its completion being 1382.[1] The scribe and illuminator—for they were one and the same person—was Elijah ben Abraham Benveniste, scion of a famous Provençal family, who began this work in 1366, when he was 41 years of age. He thus spent 16 years upon it, being 57 years at the time of its completion. Long and arduous as the task was, the result was well worthy of the time and labour spent upon it. The manuscript is an exceedingly handsome one, rich in brilliantly executed full-page arabesques of which there are thirty of various patterns and intricacy. Round their borders are inscribed sentences from the Hebrew Bible eulogizing or otherwise bearing upon the Tōrāh and its commandments. The various books of the Hebrew Bible are each provided with ornamental headings, the sole exception being the Book of Lamentations. In addition, the beginning of each pericope is also distinguished by marginal ornamentation in which the first two or three letters of the Hebrew word פרשה are framed. A Biblical lexicon precedes the text of the Bible. In addition to the arabesques already mentioned the manuscript includes a number of miniatures illustrating the Tabernacle and the sacred vessels. To these familiar objects are added two themes of an unusual kind, the maze leading to the city of Jericho, and the tents of Jacob and his wives (Pl. xxxiv, 1, 2).

The presence of a classical motif like the maze, whose actual existence in Cnossus has been brought to light by the brilliant excavations of Sir Arthur Evans, is a rare occurrence in illuminated Hebrew Bibles. The theme is, it need hardly be said, more familiar to students of Christian iconography, where its appearance in various forms, rectangular, octagonal, and circular, upon the mosaic floors of cathedrals and in the pages of manuscripts can be traced right through the Middle Ages.[2]

[1] The manuscript is now in the possession of Mr. D. S. Sassoon. It is described by him in his *Descriptive Catalogue*, London, 1932, vol. i, pp. 6–14 (no. 368).

[2] See *Dictionnaire d'Archéologie Chrétienne*, s.v. Labyrinthe. According

A miniature of the tents of Jacob and his wives is also rare although not unknown. No human figures are included, a feature characteristic of most of these Spanish and Portuguese manuscripts. A more familiar theme is that of the bunch of grapes brought back by the spies from the Holy Land, a miniature of which is found on p. 149 of the manuscript.[1]

Several pages are devoted to representations of the sacred vessels of the Tabernacle and Temple. Upon one (p. 182) is depicted an elaborately wrought Menōrāh upon a diapered background, enclosed in borders of intricate strapwork of an Oriental pattern (Pl. xxxv. 1). In the following page are assembled a number of other objects connected with the service of the Tabernacle and Temple, notably the altar, the golden Table of the Shewbread, and the rings and staves used for carrying the ark. On p. 186 we are introduced to several forms of musical instruments, which, the inscription tells us, were of the kind used by the Levites. The two silver trumpets are seen at the top. Beneath are shown three stringed instruments which represent, of course, those current at the time the manuscript

to A. B. Cook the maze evolved from the *swastika*. See his *Zeus*, i, pp. 472 ff. It would be interesting to trace the connexion of the theme of the maze with Jewish art. The scarlet thread provides the point of contact between the Bible and classical mythology. See C. Roth, *A Casale Pilgrim*, London, 1929, p. 35, for another (late) Jewish representation of the maze of Jericho. The stone labyrinths round Helsinki are variously (and curiously) called 'Ruins of Jerusalem', 'City of Nineveh', and 'Walls of Jericho'. See W. H. Mathews, *Mazes and Labyrinths*, London, 1922, p. 150.

[1] Kaufmann, op. cit., p. 273, draws attention to a miniature of the tents of Jacob and his wives in a service-book forming no. 821 of the Gunzbourg collection. The miniature pictorializes the opening words of the daily prayers—'How goodly are thy tents, O Jacob' (Num. xxiv. 5). Their *raison d'être* is easily explained when we recall how often the subjects of these two illustrations are discussed in Rabbinic literature. Some manuscript copies of the commentary of Rashī and the supercommentaries thereon contain plans and diagrams illustrating these subjects.

was written, and are not to be taken as exact reproductions of the musical instruments used some two thousand years previously. The centre of the picture is occupied by the jar of manna. On the left is the sprouting rod of Aaron (Pl. xxxv. 2).

Representations of the Tables of the Law, the mortar in which the ingredients for the incense were pounded, and a jar, possibly for the spices, are found on p. 187 of the manuscript. In the top left-hand corner we have an olive-tree planted upon a hill-side (Pl. xxxvi. 1). The inscription accompanying the picture describes it as the Mount of Olives. Its appearance among the sacred vessels demands some explanation. It may perhaps be interpreted as a pendant to the Menōrāh, for which the trees on the Mount of Olives supplied the oil. In the Hebrew Bible completed at Perpignan in 1298, now at the Bibliothèque Nationale, we find a picture of an olive-tree on the verso of the page containing a representation of the Menōrāh, thus emphasizing the connexion between the two objects.[1] The Menōrāh and the Two Tables of the Law, it may be noted, are reproduced twice, in different parts of the Sassoon manuscript. Other objects illustrated are Noah's Ark and the Urim and Thummin.

Of the beautifully executed arabesques in which this manuscript abounds the one chosen for reproduction is particularly interesting as it contains the only example of representations of living things. Within the octagonally shaped design are pictures of birds, all of the same kind and grouped in pairs (Pl. xxxvi. 2). The arabesques

[1] The Vision of Zechariah (chap. iv) supplies the main motif for these and similar miniatures. The Golden Menōrāh is there flanked on either side by an olive-tree. It may be recalled that there exists a specimen of gold glass upon which the Virgin Mary is depicted between two olive-trees. Leclercq, who reproduces this (from Garrucci's *Vetri ornati di figure*, 1858) in the *Dictionnaire d'Archéologie Chrétienne*, tom. 1, pt. 2, col. 2699, fig. 886, aptly quotes from Proclus, who interprets the two olive-trees as the Old and New Testaments respectively. Leclercq does not, however, mention the connexion of this kind of representation with the Vision described in Zechariah iv.

ILLUMINATED MANUSCRIPTS OF THE WEST

are indeed all remarkable for the vitality of their designs and the beauty of their workmanship.

The second manuscript is a Hebrew Bible in three volumes at the British Museum, bearing the numbers Oriental 2626–8. It was acquired in 1882. Next to Add. 11639, which has already been described, 'this Hebrew manuscript is the most profusely illuminated copy of the Hebrew Bible in the collection. There are richly illuminated titles to each book, and, in the Pentateuch, to each weekly section, but the skill of the artist is chiefly displayed in the decoration of the supplementary leaves containing [the 613 Commandments of the Law and the] Masoretic matter. Each page of these folios has a double border, the outer one being composed of beautiful floral designs sometimes interspersed with representations of birds in gold and colours, whilst the inner border consists of delicate pen-work in coloured ink. The headings of the rubrics, as well as the whole of the Masoretic lists and "opuscula" running round the margins, are written in letters of gold.'[1] The pages selected for reproduction are:

Vol. 1, fol. 8a. A characteristic specimen of the preliminary folios in the manuscript containing in the body of the page the list of the 613 commandments, and, within the inner border, in letters of gold, a recension of Ben Asher's treatise on the vowel-points and accents (דקדוקי הטעמים 'ס). The birds, executed in green and yellow colours, are exquisitely drawn. The ornamental work is of extraordinary delicacy and beauty, to which only a coloured plate could do even some measure of justice (Pl. xxxvii).

Fol. 182a. This page comes from the end of the same volume. It contains a portion of the textual differences between the schools of Ben Asher and Ben Naphtali. The lists are arranged with an extraordinary sense of effectiveness. The decoration possesses a luminous quality which no reproduction can fully convey. A rather peculiar feature about these lists is that they are unvocalized. As the differences between the two scholars are mainly vocalic, the usefulness of these lists is somewhat

---

[1] Quoted from G. Margoliouth, *Catalogue of the Hebrew and Samaritan Manuscripts in the British Museum*, part i, p. 35.

abridged. The scribe was possibly too good an artist to wish to spoil the fine calligraphic effect which the page displays by the insertion of vowel-points. It was the decorative value rather than the scholarly that he appears to have thought of primarily (Pl. xxxviii).

This splendid manuscript was completed at Lisbon towards the end of 1482, by Samuel ben Samuel Ibn Mūsā, the scribe, for the owner Joseph ben Judah al-Ḥakīm. From the colophon it appears likely that the scribe was also the illuminator.[1] He views his handiwork with pardonable pride and gives thanks to God for having been spared to see the completion of his task.

I now come to the last of the three Hebrew Bibles which I have chosen for special notice. The Bodleian is the fortunate owner of this masterpiece of calligraphy and the art of the illuminator. It is characteristic of the little interest displayed in Jewish art at the time that the late Dr. Neubauer dismissed the manuscript in a few lines in his Catalogue. The manuscript is known as Kennicott 1, it having at one time formed part of that famous scholar's collection. The names of both the calligrapher and illuminator are preserved in the manuscript. We learn from the colophon that this Hebrew Bible was copied at Corunna by Moses Ibn Zabara for Isaac ben Solomon de Braga. It was completed in 1476 and illuminated by Joseph Ibn Ḥayyīm. The manuscript was thus entirely the work of Jewish hands, and is easily the finest existing example of Jewish art as applied to a manuscript.

In addition to the Biblical text the manuscript contains a copy of Ḳimḥī's grammatical treatise, the *Sēpher ham-Mikhlōl*, the text being distributed at the beginning and end of the volume. As in similar copies of Spanish and Portuguese Hebrew Bibles it is in this portion of the manuscript that the artist has shown all his dazzling skill. Each page is a

---

[1] That the scribe and illuminator were one and the same person appears to be established from the phrase ידי שמואל רקמום ('the hands of Samuel adorned them') in the closing lines of the colophon.

ILLUMINATED MANUSCRIPTS OF THE WEST

masterpiece of decoration. So great is the artist's range and resourcefulness, that the illuminator rarely repeats himself.

The manuscript, which is a large quarto in format, contains 445 folios of the finest white vellum. It is in a remarkably fine state of preservation and has suffered little from the passage of centuries. There are 77 full-page illuminations in addition to some 173 smaller decorations scattered over the whole volume. The two halves of the *Sēpher ham-Mikhlōl*, which appear respectively at the beginning and end of the codex, consist each of 15 full-page illuminations in which the text of the *Mikhlōl* is embodied. The other 47 full-page illuminations are distributed in various parts of the manuscript, as title-pages, tail-pieces, and so forth.

A few historiated miniatures are to be found in the margins and elsewhere. Charming as they are they appear somewhat incongruous in a work of art whose chief merit is its pure ornament. These miniatures include representations of David, Jonah, and Phinehas. In addition, there are the usual copies of the sacred utensils.

It is in the full-page illuminations which embody the text of Ḳimḥi's grammatical treatise *Sēpher ham-Mikhlōl* that the artist displays his greatest skill and mastery, his designs flowing freely and effortlessly from his brush, and rarely repeating themselves. Another merit of this manuscript is the ideal collaboration which is everywhere shown between artist and calligrapher, whose joint labours unite to form a beautifully balanced page, in which neither is found to encroach upon the other's province. The full-page illuminations at the beginning and end of the volume are divided into two columns, tapering to arches of various architectural styles. The richness of the designs never degenerates into flamboyance, nor is their vitality marred by fantastication. The decoration is everywhere controlled by an impeccable taste. It is, I am well aware, dangerous to translate one art into terms of another, but if a personal impression be permitted, these pages remind me of the finest music (to the condition of which all art, as Pater reminds us, aspires) in their perfect combination of form and content and in the unfailing vitality of their patterns.

Of the more notable pages, artistically speaking, from this incomparable manuscript may be mentioned:

Fol. 4a. One of the richly decorated introductory pages. The superb beauty and vigour of this miniature can be appreciated even through the unsatisfactory medium of a monochrome. See Frontispiece.

Fol. 7a. Another of the introductory pages, exemplifying the skill and versatility of the artist (Pl. xxxix. 1).

Fol. 9b. The first page of Genesis. Compared with the richly decorated introductory and concluding pages, the style is somewhat restrained, the reverence with which the Biblical text was treated militating against too lavish a use of ornamentation. The Māsōrāh, it will be noted, is treated decoratively, little regard being shown for the reader who might wish to study it from this copy.

Fol. 92a. The marginal illustration is that of Phinehas, armed with shield and lance. The Castilian Bible of Moses Arragel, it may be remembered, illustrates the same theme (supra, p. 91). Phinehas plays a great role in Rabbinic literature, where his resourcefulness and prompt action in saving Israel are much lauded.

Fol. 180a. A miniature of King David in the margin. The artist draws his own conception of a king. It is a very Jewish-looking figure which he shows us, and, apparently, no mere slavish imitation of current models (Pl. xxxix 2).[1]

Fol. 305a. A charming vignette of Jonah and the whale in the margin (Pl. xl. 1).

Fol. 370a. A specimen page from the Book of Psalms. As in so many of the Christian Psalters, from which the practice may well have been borrowed, each Psalm is treated decoratively. The page is a typical example of the artist's felicitous chain-work and floral ornamentation (Pl. xl. 2).

Of the artist's elaborately executed arabesques some fine examples will be found on fols. 122b (Pl. xli. 1), 318a, and 352b (Pl. xli. 2) in the manuscript. The first of these embodies a decorative treatment of the 'Shield of David'

---

[1] The miniature bears, however, some resemblance to pictures of the King on playing-cards.

(*Māghēn Dāvīdh*),¹ a (presumably) stellar symbol, whose Jewish association can be traced back to very early times, although the same emblem is found also later in Muslim and (to a lesser extent) Christian art.²

This manuscript may well be said to represent the culminating point of the art of the Hebrew Bible. Although not the last of such manuscripts in point of date, this Bible was executed at a time when a new invention, by means of which it was possible to multiply copies of the same work cheaply, was fast ruining the vocation of calligrapher and illuminator. The illuminated manuscript in Europe had reached its apogee. From now on its history is one of rapidly declining prestige.³ The illuminated Hebrew Bible shared the fate of its Christian contemporary.⁴ But meanwhile a far more tragic fate was menacing the Jews of Spain and Portugal than the decay of illuminated Bibles. By the evil genius of Queen Isabella and Torquemada a highly cultured, cohesive, and prosperous community was reduced in the course of a few months to beggary and exile. The supremacy of Spanish Jewry, which had written so brilliant a page of history, was shattered for ever.

[1] The earliest appearance of the *Māghēn Dāvīdh* is on a very ancient Jewish seal, that of 'Yehoshua, son of Asayahu'. See S. A. Cook, op. cit., p. 46. For a *Māghēn Dāvīdh* found upon a tombstone at Tarentum assigned to the third century A.D., see H. M. Adler in *JQR* xiv, 1902, pp. 111. In modern times the 'Shield of David' has been adopted as the symbol of Jewish nationalism.

[2] For a description of this manuscript, see R. Wischnitzer-Bernstein, 'Une Bible enluminée par Joseph Ibn Hayyim', *Revue des Études Juives*, vol. 73, 1921, pp. 161–72.

[3] In striking contrast to this decline in the West was the flowering of the art of Persian and Mughal miniatures in the East in the fourteenth and fifteenth centuries, where it attained the climax of its development in the sixteenth and seventeenth centuries.

[4] The tradition of producing beautiful Hebrew Bibles was successfully maintained in the printed editions, particularly during the fifteenth century. Here, too, it is the Bibles produced in Spain and Portugal which are among the finest examples of the printer's art.

CHAPTER V
CONCLUSION

IF the reader expects to find cut and dried conclusions in this chapter, he will be disappointed. The subject bristles with too many unanswered interrogation-marks to admit of finality or easy solutions. It must suffice at this stage to indicate the main lines of approach to the problems, to map out the course roughly, and, where possible, to provide a sign-post for the traveller in this uncharted territory. Many of the problems have already been touched upon in other parts of the book, but it may perhaps be useful to assemble them here, so that a better appreciation of their value and importance can be gained.

One of the questions which await an answer is the antiquity of O.T. illustration. Evidence confirming the existence of such illustration before the Dura wall-paintings is provided by the remarkable mosaic uncovered in Malta, depicting (almost certainly) Samson and Delilah. From the discovery of a bust of the Emperor Claudius at the same villa, we are able to supply a *terminus a quo* for the date of the mosaic. Then we have the painting found at Pompeii in which the Judgement of Solomon is caricatured. Forming part of the same series is another painting in which the theme of Jonah and the whale appears to be humorously treated. Are we justified in regarding these precious relics as pointing to the existence of a nucleus of O.T. illustration, out of which there grew the more ambitious picture cycles as exemplified by the frescoes of Dura-Europos? Such an assumption would help us to explain the statement made (perhaps too emphatically) by Kraeling that the frescoes of Dura are 'undoubtedly the product of a long period of development'.[1] If we admit the possibility of such a long development amongst the Jews we come up against a difficulty. For the Talmūdh tells us that it was

---

[1] Rep. vi. 382.

CONCLUSION

in the days of Rabbi Jochanan bar Nappāḥā that wall-paintings were permitted. For reasons which I have given elsewhere in this book[1] the synagogue of Dura must have been among the earliest to be so decorated. The long period of development which Kraeling claims for these frescoes could not therefore have taken place in the synagogue. That, however, does not rule out the possibility of such art flourishing in the private home, in support of which the mosaic at Malta and (indirectly) the paintings at Pompeii may be taken to bear witness. (The custom amongst wealthy Jews in the Middle Ages of adorning their houses with paintings illustrative of the Hebrew Bible may thus have been a continuation or revival of an old tradition.) When we consider how rich the Hebrew Bible is in material for the painter's brush, it is not unreasonable to assume, from the evidence provided by the Maltese and Pompeian finds, that the Jews in the Empire, as early as the first century of the Christian Era, had turned to their own religious and historical traditions for the subjects of their art, while drawing upon the current artistic traditions of their pagan neighbours for its form.

Yet another problem is to ascertain what part the Dura frescoes played in the development of Christian art. Not least among the merits of these unique wall-paintings is that they preserve for us in so many cases the earliest surviving examples of O.T. illustration, whether Christian or Jewish. It has been suggested that both the Dura frescoes and the miniatures in Christian manuscripts go back to a common source.[2] It is interesting to note that one art historian has essayed a reconstruction of the prototype from a detailed study of a Dura fresco and a miniature in the Paris Gregory Nazianzenus (no. 510).[3] What is badly

[1] Supra, p. 57.
[2] G. Wodtke, 'Malereien der Synagoge und ihre Parallelen in der christlichen Kunst', in the *Zeitschrift für die neutestamentliche Wissenschaft*, Berlin, 1935, Band 34, 51–62.
[3] H. Buchthal, *The Miniatures of the Paris Psalter*, p. 20. The subject is the Anointing of David by Samuel.

needed is a systematic and comprehensive study of the Dura frescoes in relation to the Christian material. Some attempt in this direction has already been made by Gitta Wodtke in an interesting and suggestive article.[1] Other marked resemblances between these two types of art have been noted in this volume, more particularly in Chapter II.

A systematic collation of the Dura frescoes and the Christian material will probably reveal many more striking parallels. The origin of O.T. art had begun to exercise the minds of art historians even before the discoveries at Dura. Some of them, like Joseph Strzygowski,[2] Oskar Wulff,[3] and Henrik Cornell[4] sought to explain the preponderance of O.T. themes over subjects from the N.T. as due to Jewish prototypes.[5] The Sacrifice of Isaac, Noah's Ark, Moses striking the rock, the Three Youths in the fiery furnace, Daniel in the lions' den, Jonah and the whale, are subjects which recur regularly in the Christian catacombs of Rome. It is, moreover, significant that so many of the earliest Christian illuminated manuscripts which have come down to us, like the Cotton Genesis, the Quedlinburg fragments, the Vienna Genesis, the P^eshīttā version in Paris, and the Ashburnham Pentateuch, are copies of the whole or parts of the O.T. If it could be established that the Jews came first with pictorial representations from the Hebrew Bible, then this partiality for O.T. subjects would point to the probability that the early Christians, amongst whom were so many converted Jews, borrowed from the current Jewish picture cycles, just as they had no qualms in weaving other Jewish elements into the texture of their

---

[1] In the above-mentioned article.
[2] *Orient oder Rom?* Vienna, 1901, pp. 32–9.
[3] *Altchristliche und byzantinische Kunst*, i, Berlin, 1914, pp. 7 f; 68 f.
[4] *Biblia Pauperum*, Stockholm, 1925, p. 121.
[5] E. Bevan, *Holy Images*, pp. 101-2, touches briefly upon this curious 'predominance of pictures illustrating Old Testament Stories over pictures of the story of Jesus'. One interesting reason which he suggests is that there 'must have been some feeling that in itself the visible representation of the holy was wrong' (ibid., p. 102).

CONCLUSION

new faith.[1] We know that Christianity readily took over and adapted some of the symbols and *motifs* of Judaism.[2] We even find the Midhrāsh laid under tribute by Christian art.[3] There is thus no reason for suggesting that the early Christians would fail to make use of the Jewish corpus of Biblical illustration if it preceded their own. On the other hand, there are some weighty objections against the thesis that the Jews borrowed their picture-sets from the early Christians. In the first place, the Jews, once Christianity broke away from Rabbinic Judaism, held themselves aloof from the Christian community. It would therefore have offended their pride to take over their religious art from the Christians. Secondly, it seems clear from what has

---

[1] Hans Lietzmann, *The Founding of the Church Universal*, London, 1938, p. 186, poses the problem, but leaves the answer open. He says: 'Thus the question arises [in view of the wall-paintings at Dura-Europos] whether the Christians possibly borrowed, not only these prayers, but also the pictorial representations from the Jews.' A more definite position in favour of the thesis that the early Christians borrowed from the Jews, in the light of the newly found wall-paintings at Dura, is taken up by Clark Hopkins. See his article 'Jewish Prototypes of Early Christian Art', in the *Illustrated London News* of July 29, 1933, pp. 189–91.

[2] S. A. Cook, op. cit., p. 225: 'Christianity inherited the archaeological characteristics of Judaism as regards the symbols and *motifs* which it accepted or rejected.' Cook also notes the retention of Jewish burial lamps (but with Christian mottoes), and the assimilation of the vine *motif* to Christian art and doctrine (ibid., p. 226).

[3] The pictorial treatment of Lamech in Christian illuminated manuscripts is a case in point. He is represented as shooting Cain, a detail which derives, directly or indirectly, from Rabbinic exegesis. The late M. R. James, while recognizing the Jewish tradition of this legend, ingeniously sought to explain its appearance in Christian art as due to a lost Greek apocryphon of Lamech. See his Roxburghe Club publication, *Illustrations of the Book of Genesis* (Egerton 1894), Oxford, 1921, pp. 24 f. See also his introduction in *A Book of Old Testament Illustrations*, Cambridge, 1927, p. 15. The Jewish legend regarding Lamech was already known to Jerome. See L. Rayger's article 'Kain und Abel' in O. Schmitt's *Reallexikon zur deutschen Kunstgeschichte*, vol. i, 1937, coll. 22–4.

been said above, that the Jews appear already to have possessed a nucleus of O.T. illustration of their own, even before the beginnings of Christian art. There is thus a *prima facie* case in favour of the Jewish priority of O.T. art, with its corollary of Christian borrowing from it. The view that the Jews materially influenced the development of Christian art has not been allowed to pass unchallenged. O. M. Dalton, for example, explicitly denies Jewish influence upon Christian art in respect of either style or form, although he advances no reasons in support of his contention.[1] Karl Künstle dismisses summarily the views of Wulff upon this subject.[2] At this stage, an hypothesis in favour of the Jewish origin of O.T. illustration can only be a provisional one. Such an hypothesis can only be regarded as 'a temporary bridge' (in the apt phrase of Sir James Frazer), which fresh knowledge may either demolish or strengthen.

Another important element in the evolution of Jewish and Christian iconography must not be overlooked. I refer to the influence which pagan art exerted upon them both. A subject like Adam and Eve in its earliest forms shows its dependence upon the classical representation of Hercules and the Golden Apples of the Hesperides and of Jason and Medea. Similarly, the theme of the Sacrifice of Isaac is greatly indebted to the pagan pictures of the Sacrifice of Iphigenia.[3] The paintings in the Jewish catacomb on the Via Appia reflect, according to Pater Frey, pagan influences, especially of Orphism.[4] As for the frescoes at

[1] *East Christian Art*, Oxford, 1925, p. 9. 'Jewish influence on Christian art', he says, 'was exerted rather through the Hellenised Jews of the dispersion in Alexandria, Antioch, and other foreign cities; it did not affect the style or form but only certain aspects of the matter and spirit.'

[2] *Ikonographie der christlichen Kunst*, Band i, Freiburg im Breisgau, 1928, p. 23.

[3] See F. Saxl, 'Pagan Sacrifice in the Italian Renaissance', in the *Journal of the Warburg Institute*, vol. ii, no. 4, p. 347.

[4] See T. Gaster's review of the *Corpus Inscriptionum Judaicarum*, in the *Journal of the Royal Asiatic Society*, 1939, p. 134.

CONCLUSION

Dura-Europos, Professor Rostovtzeff, than whom there can be no greater authority, says, 'the system of decoration in the synagogue is strikingly similar to that of all the pagan temples of Dura and to that of the Christian church'.[1] The subjects were of course different, but not the style or treatment, although Rostovtzeff notes as a distinctive feature the fluid form of narration employed in the synagogue frescoes. Moreover, while Rostovtzeff emphasizes the pervasive influence upon the Durene frescoes generally of a Hellenistic art in which were blended Oriental elements, he points out at the same time how this Oriental character has profoundly modified some of the accessories in these paintings. The architectural background and the draperies, for example, have shed their organic function and have become severely formalized.[2] But the debt which the iconography of both the Old and New Testaments owes to Hellenism is paramount and fundamental.

There remains the question of the extent to which the miniatures in the Hebrew manuscripts are related to the wall-paintings at Dura and the mosaics in the ancient synagogues. The subject is one upon which, in our present state of knowledge, it would be foolish to dogmatize. We can only offer the reader some tentative suggestions, which are made with a due sense of their provisional character. So many of the intermediate links in the chain of the Jewish tradition of Old Testament illustration are missing that the task of relating the miniatures in the Hebrew manuscripts to their prototypes is one of great difficulty. Many of our problems might have been brought nearer to solution had the frescoes at Dura been preserved intact. The survival of so few mosaics from the ancient synagogues, and the complete disappearance of the paintings depicting themes from the Hebrew Bible with which Jews were known to adorn the walls of their houses, have not rendered the task of reconstructing the material any easier.

[1] *Dura-Europos and its Art*, p. 114.   [2] op. cit., p. 81.

CONCLUSION

A comparison of the illuminated Hebrew Bibles and *Haggādhōth* with the wall-paintings at Dura reveals the fact that many of the subjects illustrated in the synagogue reappear in the pages of the Hebrew manuscripts. The Sacrifice of Isaac, the Discovery of the Infant Moses, Pharaoh interviewing the Jewish Midwives, Moses and the Burning Bush, the Wells of Elim, the Crossing of the Red Sea, the Story of Esther, the picture of the Restored Temple, are subjects which are shared both by frescoes in the synagogues and miniatures in the manuscripts. What is more, it is not only the choice of subject that distinguishes these two phases of Jewish religious art. A closer examination reveals further points of contact, which are not without their significance. Certain of the representations betray not only an identity of subject but also a similarity of treatment. This is noticeable in the handling of Pharaoh interviewing the midwives, the Discovery of the Infant Moses by Pharaoh's daughter, the Passage of the Israelites through the Red Sea, and, possibly, the Triumph of Mordecai over Haman.

Of these four subjects, the first three are regularly reproduced in illustrated copies of the *Haggādhāh*. Other points of contact between the *Haggādhōth* and the frescoes of Dura-Europos may be noted.[1] Representations of the Wells of Elim and the Temple Restored are to be found in both manuscript and fresco. Even more striking is the appearance of the themes of Moses unrolling the Law and of Joshua and the Angel on two successive pages in the Second *Haggādhāh* of Nuremberg, and, next to each other, on the central panel in the synagogue at Dura.[2] So many points

[1] The possession by Kaufmann of a fragment of a *Haggādhāh* with rudimentary illustrations, obtained from the G*e*nīzāh in Egypt, led him significantly to seek in the East the source of illustrated *Haggādhōth*. The two subjects illustrated, both non-representational, were the *Maṣṣāh* (unleavened bread) and *mārōr* (bitter herbs). See Kaufmann's note in *JQR* x, (1898), p. 381.

[2] The two themes are also found depicted side by side in Christian manuscripts of Byzantine origin or exhibiting Byzantine influences.

of contact cannot be dismissed as a mere matter of chance. They would seem to imply the existence of an independent tradition of representational art amongst the Jews. Such an explanation is more in accordance with probability than to suppose that this tradition lapsed completely and then, after the passage of many centuries, revived again as a kind of offshoot of Christian art, without having its roots in the past. Moreover, this latter supposition would not account satisfactorily for the many points of resemblance between the ancient frescoes of Dura-Europos and the miniatures in the medieval Jewish manuscripts. It must be admitted, however, that the theory of a continuous tradition of Jewish iconography can only so far remain a suggestion, for the intermediate links are sadly lacking. Until they are established, we should be wise to suspend our judgement. A careful collation of the Jewish material with its Christian counterpart would be the first step towards clarifying the problem. A task which especially requires doing is to find out whether the frescoes at Dura-Europos influenced the later iconography of the Jews directly or only through the medium of Christian exemplars.

The arguments in favour of Jewish priority of O.T. illustration do not minimize the influence which the Christian illuminated manuscripts exerted upon the Jews in medieval times. Whatever the debt early Christian iconography may have owed to Jewish art, the picture is reversed when we come to the Middle Ages. Here we find the Christian influence upon Jewish manuscripts all-pervasive. The Jews not only borrowed their general scheme of decoration from Christian art but also drew largely upon its iconography, in some cases adapting the illustrations to suit their own requirements.[1] On the other

---

[1] One of the most striking cases of such adaptation is the miniature in the British Museum MS. Add. 27210 (Pl. xxxi) where a picture of Moses and his family leaving Midian for Egypt is obviously patterned upon the representation so familiar in Christian art of the Flight of the Holy Family into Egypt. In later times we find Michelangelo's

hand, it is clear that the Jews in the Middle Ages did not restrict themselves solely to the Christian corpus. For they included in their repertory such specifically Jewish subjects as the Tents of Jacob, Aaron lighting the Menōrāh, the Bunch of Grapes carried by the Spies from the Holy Land, the Death of Moses, and the Temple Restored.

The history of Jewish religious art has been a chequered one. Like Christian and Muslim art, it has not escaped from the destructive zeal of iconoclasts. It has suffered, too, from the intermittent opposition of Rabbinical authority and from the constant migrations of the Jewish people. For art, more than most activities of the human race, needs to take deep root in the soil before it can produce sturdy shoots. It is for this reason that some people have gone so far as to deny to the Jews a distinctive art since the days of the Diaspora. These pages, and more especially the plates, may perhaps do something to correct this conception.

It must, however, be conceded that compared with those grand achievements in stone, glass, metal, and paint, which form such imperishable monuments of Christian civilization, Jewish religious art remains circumscribed in scope and limited in achievement. With the bright exception of the wall-paintings at Dura, the extant body of early Jewish art remains too scanty and fragmentary for its value and importance to be adequately assessed. The frescoes in the synagogues at Dura are not without artistic merit. Yet even here the most notable fact about them is the way in which their spiritual intensity so often transcends the technical limitations of the artist. Some of the frescoes, like the Esther frieze, for example, admirably convey a

---

Jeremiah impressed into the service of a printed *Haggādhāh* (*Mantua*, 1560) to do duty for a representation of Rabbi 'Ăḳībhā. Other examples of Christian influences upon Jewish art are given by E. Panofsky, 'Giotto and Maimonides in Avignon', *Journal of the Walters Art Gallery*, vol. iv, Baltimore, 1941, pp. 26–44, note 18. He notes especially a relief upon a Jewish tombstone 'manifestly influenced by representations of the "Death of the Virgin"' (ibid., p. 43, note 18).

sense of vitality and dramatic force. The noble 'portrait-panel' of Moses reading the Law, which breathes such spiritual exaltation and serene dignity, easily dominates them all. In this connexion it should be remembered that in order to appreciate these paintings best, they should be envisaged in their original surroundings. Possibly the reason why some people have been disappointed in them is because they have judged them apart from their *milieu*. A medium like fresco-painting, too, must not be judged from the same viewpoint as oil-paintings.

But Jewish religious art, with exceptions here and there, shines most in the field of pure ornament. It is in the splendid illuminated codices of the Hebrew Bible, mostly of Spanish or Portuguese origin, in which little or no representational art appears, where one aspect of the Jewish artistic genius is seen at its best. The finest examples in this class can challenge comparison with the corresponding products of Christian and Islamic art. In such manuscripts as the Kennicott and Lisbon Bibles we find the scribe and illuminator collaborating in the production of a perfect work of art. Grace of design faultlessly executed goes hand in hand with the decorative effects of an alphabet which successive generations of scribes had wrought into an instrument of incomparable beauty. In these masterpieces the Hebrew Bible had found a setting to match its contents.

I. ADDITIONAL NOTE ON THE WELLS OF ELIM
(*pp. 39–40*)

It is interesting to find that the Ḳur'ān associates the miracle of the twelve gushing streams with the incident of Moses striking the rock: 'And when Moses asked for water for his people, We said: Smite with thy staff the rock. And there gushed out therefrom twelve springs (so that) each tribe knew their drinking place.' (*Sūrah* ii. 60. M. Pickthall's translation.)

II. ADDITIONAL NOTE ON THE BAR-YOKHNĪ, LEVIATHAN AND SHŌR HAB-BĀR
(*pp. 77–8, nos. 3, 5, 6*)

Rabbinic legend assigns these monsters to the fifth and sixth days of the Creation. It is thus possible that the miniatures nos. 3, 5, and 6 were designed to illustrate some of the events recorded in the first chapter of Genesis. (The first two miniatures in the series, representing the zodiac, and the sun, moon and stars, may also owe their *raison d'être* to the same cause.) Bar-Yokhnī is only another name for the fabulous Zīz, about which the Aggādhāh has so much to say. We are told in the Babylonian Talmūdh (*Bᵉkhōrōth* 57*b*) that the egg of a Zīz having been accidentally dropped, it 'flooded sixty cities and shattered three hundred cedar trees'. From the same source we learn that the Bar-Yokhnī was identified with the ostrich mentioned in Job xxxix. 13. L. Ginzberg brilliantly translates Bar-Yokhnī by 'son of the nest', deriving yokhnī from the Arabic *wuknah*, 'a nest'. (See his article 'Bar Yokni' in *JE*, ii, p. 512.) The Shōr hab-bār appears to be a variant of the more familiar Behemoth. The flesh of these three monsters was to be reserved for the righteous in the world to come (presumably for their last meal, before they were turned into pure spirit). For the legends associated with these beasts, see L. Ginzberg, *The Legends of the Jews*, vol. i, pp. 26–31; and vol. v, pp. 41–5, notes 116–46. The Zīz has incidentally achieved the distinction of a dissertation to itself—by a German scholar. See J. H. Wolfius, *Dissertatio de portentosae magnitudinis ave* זיז שדי, Leipzig, 1683. (Ginzberg, l.c., vol. v, p. 46, note 129.)

BIBLIOGRAPHY AND ABBREVIATIONS

The bibliography makes no attempt to be exhaustive. With a few exceptions, it is confined to the books and articles quoted in the text and notes. The reader will find several useful articles under their appropriate headings in the *Jewish Encyclopedia* and in the uncompleted *Encyclopaedia Judaica*. Only a selection has been given of the growing literature upon the wall-paintings of the synagogue at Dura-Europos. It has not been considered necessary to list the large number of preliminary reports and communications upon this subject, the gist of most of them having been absorbed into the later books and articles. A bibliography of this material up to 1938 will be found on p. 6, note 2, of du Mesnil's recent work, *Les Peintures de la Synagogue de Doura-Europos*. From the vast literature upon Christian art a few books have been chosen which refer, however briefly, to the Jewish aspects of the subject.

Abraham ben Judah Ibn Ḥayyīm. 'An old Portuguese work on manuscript illustration' [by Abraham ben Judah Ibn Ḥayyīm, edited, with a translation, by D. S. Blondheim], *JQR*, N.S. xix, 1928, pp. 97–135.
—— 'Livro de como se fazen as cores' [the text of Ibn Ḥayyīm's Judaeo-Portuguese manual transcribed into Latin characters, by D. S. Blondheim], *Memorial Volumes to Professor H. A. Todd*, vol. i. New York, 1930.
Abrahams (I.). 'Recent Criticism of the Letter of Aristeas', *JQR*, xiv, 1902, pp. 321–42.
—— *Jewish Life in the Middle Ages*. Second edition. London, 1932.
Adler (E. N.). 'A Hebrew MS. illustrated by Giotto', *JQR*, xi, 1899, pp. 679–82.
—— 'Jewish Art.' [A brief sketch of the history of Jewish miniature painting, being pp. 37–49 of *Occident and Orient . . . Studies in honour of M. Gaster's 80th Birthday*, London, 1936.]
Albright (F. W.). *The Archaeology of Palestine and the Bible*. New York, 1933.
Ameisenowa (Z.). *Biblja hebrajska xiv-go wieku w Krakowie i jej dekoracja malarska*. Kraków, 1929.
—— 'Bestiarius w Biblji Hebrajskiej xiii-go wieku' [i.e. 'A Bestiary in a Hebrew Bible of the thirteenth century'], *Miesięcznik Żydowski*, Warsaw, 1933.
—— 'Das messianische Gastmahl der Gerechten in einer hebräischen Bibel aus dem XIII. Jahrhundert', *MGWJ*, Band 79, 1935, pp. 409–22.
—— 'Eine spanisch-jüdische Bilderbibel um 1400', *MGWJ*, Jahrg. 81, 1937, pp. 193–209.
—— 'The Tree of Life in Jewish Iconography', *Journal of the Warburg Institute*, vol. ii, no. 4, 1939, pp. 326–45.

Aristeas. *See* Swete (H. B.); Thackeray (H. St. J.).
Arnold (*Sir* Thomas Walker). *Old and New Testaments in Muslim Religious Art*. London, 1932 [*Schweich Lectures*, 1928.]
Arzē L'bhānōn. *See* Midhrāsh.
Aubert (M.). 'Le Peintre de la Synagogue de Doura', *Gazette des Beaux-Arts*, 1938 (ii), pp. 1–14.

Bernheimer (C.). *Codices Hebraici Bybliothecae Ambrosianae*. Florentiae, 1933. [*Fontes Ambrosianae*, 5.]
Bevan (E.). *Holy Images. An Enquiry into Idolatry and Image-Worship in Ancient Paganism and in Christianity*. London, 1940. [Part of *Gifford Lectures*.]
Beyer (H. W.) and Lietzmann (H.). *Die jüdische Katakombe der Villa Torlonia im Rom*. Berlin and Leipzig, 1930.
Bible. *Biblia (Antiguo Testamento). Traducida del hebreo al castellano por Rabi Mosé Arragel de Guadalfajara* (1422–33?) *y publicada por el Duque de Berwick y de Alba*. 2 vols. Madrid, 1920, 1922. [An edition of the Roxburghe Club.]
—— *A Book of Old Testament Illustrations of the middle of the thirteenth century... now in the Pierpont Morgan Library at New York. Described by Sidney C. Cockerell.... With an introduction by Montague Rhodes James*. Cambridge, 1927. [An edition of the Roxburghe Club. The introduction consists of the *Sandars Lectures for 1924* by M. R. James on 'Illustration in the Old Testament'.]
Biebel (F. M.). 'The Mosaics of Hammam Lif', *Art Bulletin*, xviii, no. 4, 1936, pp. 541–51.
Blau (L.). *Studien zum althebräischen Buchwesen*. Strassburg, 1902.
Blondheim (D. S.). *See* Abraham ben Judah Ibn Ḥayyīm.
Braunholtz (H. J.). *See* Strzygowski (J.).
Buchthal (H.). *The Miniatures of the Paris Psalter. A Study in Middle Byzantine Painting*. Warburg Institute: London, 1938.

Cabrol (F.) and Leclercq (H.). *Dictionnaire d'Archéologie chrétienne et de Liturgie*. Paris, 1907, &c.
Cohn-Wiener (E.). *Die jüdische Kunst*. Berlin, 1929.
Colson (F. H.). *See* Philo Judaeus.
Cook (A. B.). *Zeus: A Study in Ancient Religion*. 3 vols. Cambridge, 1914–40.
Cook (S. A.). *The Religion of Ancient Palestine in the Light of Archaeology*. London, 1930. [*Schweich Lectures*, 1925.]
Cornell (A.). *Biblia Pauperum*. Stockholm, 1925.
Coulton (G. G.). *Art and the Reformation*. Oxford, 1928.
Cumont (F.). 'Catacombes juives de Rome', *Syria*, 1921, pp. 145–8.

Dalton (O. M.). *See* London—*British Museum*; Strzygowski (J.).
—— *East Christian Art: A survey of the monuments*. Oxford, 1925.

Ehrenstein (T.). *Das alte Testament im Bilde.* Wien, 1923.
—— *Über die Fresken der Synagoge von Dura-Europos.* Wien, 1937.
Eisler (R.). 'Deux sculptures de l'antiquité classique représentant des juifs', *Aréthuse*, vol. vii (1930), pp. 29–38.
Encylopaedia Judaica [in German]. Vols. 1–10 [A–L]. Berlin, 1928–34.
Excavations at Dura-Europos. Report of sixth season (1932–3). Yale University Press: New Haven, 1936.
[Quoted as Rep. vi. Pp. 309–95, which have also been issued separately, contain the 'Preliminary Report on the Synagogue at Dura', with contributions by C. H. Kraeling, H. F. Pearson, and others.]

Fooner (M.). 'Joel ben Simeon, Illuminator of Hebrew MSS. in the XVth century', *JQR*, N.S. xxvii (1937), pp. 217–32.
Frey (J.-B.). *Corpus Inscriptionum Judaicarum.* Città del Vaticano, 1956.
—— 'La question des images chez les Juifs à la lumière des récentes découvertes', *Biblica*, xv, 1934, pp. 265–300.

Gaster (M.). *Hebrew Illuminated Bibles of the IXth and Xth centuries (Codices Or. Gaster, Nos. 150 and 151).* London, 1901. [Reprinted from *The Proceedings of the Society of Biblical Archaeology*, June, 1900.]
—— *The Samaritans. Their History, Doctrines and Literature.* London, 1925. [*Schweich Lectures*, 1923.]
Gebhardt (O. von). *The Miniatures of the Ashburnham Pentateuch.* Edited by O. von Gebhardt. [The English of the introduction and descriptive text by C. R. Gregory.] London, Berlin printed, 1883.
Ginzberg (L.). *The Legends of the Jews.* 7 vols. Philadelphia, 1909–38.
Golde (M.). 'Eine altkastilische Prachtbibel', *Jahrbuch für Geschichte und Literatur*, 1926.
Goodenough (E. R.). *By Light, Light. The mystic Gospel of Hellenistic Judaism.* Yale University Press: New Haven, 1935.
Gottheil (R.). 'Some Hebrew Manuscripts in Cairo' [including descriptions of a number of Karaite Hebrew illuminated Bibles, and an illustrated Western Hebrew Bible since lost], *JQR*, xvii, pp. 609–55.
Guide. See London—*British Museum*.

Haggādhāh. *Die Haggadah von Sarajevo. Eine spanisch-jüdische Bilderhandschrift des Mittelalters.* Von Dav. Heinr. Müller und Julius v. Schlosser. Nebst einem Anhange (*Zur Geschichte der jüdischen Handschriftenillustration.* Von David Kaufmann). Wien, 1898.
—— *Die Darmstädter Pessach-Haggadah. Codex Orientalis 8 der Landesbibliothek zu Darmstadt aus dem vierzehnten Jahrhundert, herausgegeben und erläutert von Bruno Italiener unter Mitwirkung von Aron Freimann, August L. Mayer und Adolf Schmidt, mit einer Gesamtbibliographie der illustrierten Haggadah.* 2 vols. Leipzig, 1927–8. Vol. 1 contains the *Textband*; vol. 2, the *Tafelband*. [For a review of this edition, *see* Marx (A.).]

Herbert (J. A.). *Illuminated Manuscripts.* London, 1911.
Higger (M.). See *Sōph^erīm.*
Hill (*Sir* George Francis). See London—*British Museum.*
Hoerning (R.). *British Museum Karaite MSS.* London, 1889. [Includes a facsimile of the Biblical MS. Or. 2540.]
Hopkins (Clark). 'Jewish Prototypes of Early Christian Art?', *Illustrated London News,* 29 July, 1933, pp. 188–91.

James (M. R.). *See* Bible.
James (M. R.) and Jenkins (C.). *A Descriptive Catalogue of the Manuscripts in the Library of Lambeth Palace.* 5 pts. Cambridge, 1930–2.
JE. Jewish Encyclopedia.
Josephus Flavius. *Josephus. With an English translation by H. St. John Thackeray* [*and Ralph Marcus*]. London, 1906. [In progress. *Loeb Classical Library.*]
JPOS. Journal of the Palestine Oriental Society.
JQR. Jewish Quarterly Review.
—— N.S. New Series.
Juster (J.). *Les Juifs dans l'empire romain.* 2 vols. Paris, 1914.

Kaufmann (D.). *See* Haggādhāh.
—— 'Art in the Synagogue', *JQR,* ix (1897), pp. 254–69.
—— 'Sens et l'origine des symboles tumulaires de l'Ancien Testament dans l'art chrétien primitif', *Revue des Études Juives,* vol. 14, 1887, pp. 33–48; 217–53.
Kenyon (*Sir* Frederic G.). *The Bible and Archaeology.* London, 1940.
Kohl (H.) and Watzinger (C.). *Antike Synagogen in Galiläa.* Leipzig, 1916.
Kohut (A.). *See* Nathan ben Jehiel.
Kraeling (C. H.). See *Excavations at Dura-Europos.*
Künstle (K.). *Ikonographie der christlichen Kunst.* 2 vols. Freiburg im Breisgau, 1928 (Band 1), 1926 (Band 2).

Leveen (J.). *See* London—*British Museum.*
Lietzmann (H.). *The Founding of the Church Universal.* London, 1938.
London—*British Museum.* See also Hoerning (R.).
—— *Catalogue of the Hebrew and Samaritan Manuscripts.* Pts. i–iii, by G. Margoliouth. Pt. iv (Indexes, Accessions, &c.), by J. Leveen. London, 1899–1935.
—— *Catalogue of the Greek Coins of Palestine* [*in the British Museum*], by G. F. Hill. London, 1914.
—— *A Guide to the Early Christian and Byzantine Antiquities in the Department of British and Mediaeval Antiquities.* [By O. M. Dalton.] Second Edition. London, 1921.

Maisler (B.). 'The Excavations at Sheikh Ibreiq, Beth She'arim, 1936–7', *JPOS*, xviii, 1938.
Margoliouth (G.). *See* London—*British Museum*.
—— 'Hebrew Illuminated MSS.', *JQR*, xx (1908), pp. 118–44.
—— 'An ancient illuminated Hebrew MS. at the British Museum' [Add. 11639], *JQR*, xvii, pp. 193–7.
Marx (A.). 'The Darmstadt Haggadah, with notes on illuminated Haggadah MSS.' [A review of Italiener's edition, including a short account of illuminated copies of the Haggādhāh in the Library of the Jewish Theological Seminary, New York], *JQR*, N.S. xix (1928–9), pp. 1–16.
Matthews (W. H.). *Mazes and Labyrinths*. London, 1922.
Mesnil du Buisson (*Comte* du). 'Les Peintures de la Synagogue de Doura-Europos', *Revue Biblique*, xliii (1934), pp. 105–19.
—— 'Les Nouvelles Découvertes de la Synagogue de Doura-Europos', *Revue Biblique*, xliii (1934), pp. 546–63.
—— *Les Peintures de la Synagogue de Doura-Europos 245–56 après J.-C.* Roma, 1939. [A bibliography of the subject (up to 1938) is given on p. 6, note 2.]
MGWJ. *Monatsschrift für die Geschichte und Wissenschaft des Judentums.*
Midhrāsh. דברי הימים של משה רבינו ע״ה [Dibhrē hay-yāmīm shel Mōsheh Rabbēnū. Miscellaneous pieces, including the Midhrāsh P^eṭīrath Mōsheh, on the death of Moses]. Constantinople, 1516.
—— ספר ארזי לבנון [Arzē L^ebhānōn. A collection of mainly Midhrāshic pieces, including *Midrash Kōnēn*]. Venice, 1601.
—— בית המדרש [Bēth ham-Midhrāsh. A collection of Midhrāshīm, including the *Midrash Kōnēn*, and *P^eṭīrath Mōsheh*, on the death of Moses]. Edited by A. Jellinek. 4 pts. Leipzig, 1853–5.
Müller (D. H.). *See* Haggādhāh.
Müller (N.). *Die jüdische Katakombe am Monteverde zu Rom.* Leipzig, 1912.
Munkácsi (E.). *Miniatúrművészet Italiakönyvtáraiban. Héber Kódeszek.* [A work in Hungarian upon Hebrew illuminated MSS. in libraries in Italy.] Budapest, (1938).

Nathan ben Jehiel. *Aruch completum*. [A Talmūdhic lexicon. Edited by A. Kohut.] 8 vols. Vienna, New York, 1878–92.
A supplementary volume, edited by S. Krauss and others, appeared in Vienna in 1937.
Neuss (W.). *Das Buch Ezechiel in der Kunst.* Münster, 1912.

Omont (H.). 'Peintures de l'ancien Testament dans un manuscrit syriaque [Ms. syriaque 341 de la Bibliothèque Nationale] du VIIe ou VIIIe siècle.' Paris, 1909. [Extrait des *Monuments et Mémoires* publiées par l'Académie des Inscriptions et Belles-Lettres.]

Panofsky (E.). 'Giotto and Maimonides in Avignon', *Journal of the Walters Art Gallery*, vol. iv. Baltimore, 1941, pp. 26–44.
Pearson (H. F.). See *Excavations at Dura-Europos*.
PEFQS. Palestine Exploration Fund. Quarterly Statement.
Philo Judaeus. *Philo*. With an English translation by F. H. Colson and G. H. Whittaker. London, 1929, &c. [In progress. *Loeb Classics*.]

Reifenberg (A.). *Denkmäler der jüdischen Antike*. Berlin, 1937.
Rep. vi. See *Excavations at Dura-Europos*.
Rimon. Hebrew Art Magazine. Edited by Rachel Vishnitzer. Nos. 1–6. London, 1924.
Romanoff (P.). 'A Family of Illuminators in the Time of the Second Temple', *JQR*, N.S. xxvi (1935), pp. 29–35.
Rosenau (H.). 'Some Aspects of the Pictorial influence of the Jewish Temple', *PEFQS*, July, 1936, pp. 157–62.
Rostovtzeff (M.). 'Die Synagoge von Dura' (*Römische Quartalschrift*, xlii (1934), pp. 208–18).
—— 'Dura and the problem of Parthian Art', *Yale Classical Studies*, vol. v, 1935, pp. 157–304.
—— *Dura-Europos and Its Art*. Oxford, 1938.

Sassoon (D. S.). אהל דוד (Ohel Dawid). *Descriptive Catalogue of the Hebrew and Samaritan Manuscripts in the Sassoon Library, London*. 2 vols. London, 1932.
Saxl (F.). 'Pagan Sacrifice in the Italian Renaissance', *Journal of the Warburg Institute*, ii (1939), pp. 346–67.
Schlosser (J. von). See Haggādhāh.
Schmitt (O.). *Reallexikon zur deutschen Kunstgeschichte*. Vol. i. Stuttgart, 1937.
Sloane (J. C.). 'The Torah Shrine in the *Ashburnham Pentateuch*', *JQR*, N.S. xxv (1934), pp. 1–12.
Sōphᵉrīm. מסכת סופרים [The tractate Sōphᵉrīm, followed by the Midrash Sōphᵉrīm and Sōphᵉrīm II. Edited by M. Higger]. [New York, 1937.]
Stassoff (W.) and Günzburg (D.). *L'Ornement hébraïque*. [Plates, with brief descriptions, mainly of illuminated Hebrew Bibles acquired by the Imperial Library of St. Petersburg from Abraham Firkovich.] Berlin, 1905.
Strzygowski (J.). *Der Bilderkreis des griechischen Physiologus* [including a reproduction of a Smyrna MS. of Kosmas Indikopleustes]. Leipzig, 1899.
—— *Orient oder Rom? Beiträge zur Geschichte der spätantiken und frühchristlichen Kunst*. Leipzig, 1901.
—— *Origin of Christian Church Art*. Translated by O. M. Dalton and H. J. Braunholtz. Oxford, 1923.
Sukenik (E. L.). *The Ancient Synagogue of Beth Alpha*. Jerusalem and London, 1932.

Sukenik (E. L.). *Ancient Synagogues in Palestine and Greece.* London, 1932. [*Schweich Lectures*, 1930.]
—— 'The Ezekiel Panel', *JPOS*, vol. 18, 1938, pp. 1–6.
Swarzenski (G.) and Schilling (R.). *Die illuminierten Handschriften und Einzelminiaturen des Mittelalters und der Renaissance in Frankfurter Besitz.* Frankfurt am Main, 1929.
Swete (H. B.). *Introduction to the Old Testament in Greek.* With an Appendix containing the Letter of Aristeas edited by H. St. J. Thackeray. Cambridge, 1914.

Talmūdh, *of Babylon.* תלמוד בבלי [Talmūdh Babhlī. The Babylonian Talmūdh]. 25 vols. Wilna, 1880–6. [The best edition.]
Talmūdh, *of Jerusalem.* תלמוד ירושלמי [Talmūdh Yᵉrushalmī. The Jerusalem Talmūdh]. Krotoschin, 1866.
תרביץ [Tarbīṣ. A Hebrew periodical]. Jerusalem, 1929, &c. [In progress.]
Thackeray (H. St. J.). *See* Josephus Flavius; Swete (H. B.).
—— 'Translation of the Letter of Aristeas', *JQR*, xv (1903), pp. 337–91.
Thompson (Sir Edward Maunde). *Greek and Latin Palaeography.* Clarendon Press: Oxford, 1912.
Thomson (P.). *Palästina und seine Kultur in fünf Jahrtausenden.* Leipzig, 1931.
Todd (H. A.). *Memorial volumes to Professor H. A. Todd.* 2 vols. New York, 1930.
Tychsen (O. G.). 'Von den mit künstlich geschriebenen Randfiguren gezierten hebräischen biblischen Handschriften', *Repertorium für biblische und morgenländische Litteratur.* Leipzig, 1778.

***One of the first Christian scholars to describe the figured Māsōrāh.*

Vishnitzer (R.). See Wischnitzer-Bernstein (R.).

Whittaker (G. H.). *See* Philo Judaeus.
Wischnitzer-Bernstein (R.). *See* Rimon.
—— *Gestalten und Symbole der jüdischen Kunst.* Berlin, 1935.
—— 'Haggadah-Illustration', *Encyclopaedia Judaica*, Band 7.
—— 'Illuminated Haggadahs', *JQR*, N.S. xiii (1922), pp. 204 ff.
—— 'Une Bible enluminée par Joseph ibn Hayyim', *Revue des Études Juives*, vol. 73, 1921, pp. 161–72.
—— 'Zur jüdischen Kunstforschung', *MGWJ*, 1931, nos. 1–2.
Wodtke (G.). 'Malereien der Synagoge in Dura und ihre Parallelen in der christlichen Kunst', *Zeitschrift für die neutestamentliche Wissenschaft*, Band 34, 1935, pp. 51–62.
Wulff (O.). *Altchristliche und byzantinische Kunst.* 2 vols. Berlin, 1914.

INDEX I

GENERAL INDEX

This index is for the most part confined to names. For the subjects discussed the reader should consult the running analysis at the beginning of the book.
The following abbreviations are used: *T.B.* (Babylonian Talmūdh); *T.Y.* (Talmūdh of Jerusalem).

Aaron ben Moses Ben Asher, 113.
Abbūn, *Rabbi*, 12.
'Ăbhōdhāh Zārāh (*T.Y.*), 12, 13^1, 56–7.
Abraham ben Judah Ibn Ḥayyim, 85.
Abraham ben Mē'īr Ibn Ezra, 81, 93.
Abrahams (I.), 5, 8, 60^1.
Adler (E. N.), 99^3.
Adler (H. M.), 117^1.
Ameisenowa (Z.), 1, 25,$^{1, 2, 3}$, 27, 63^1, 65$^{1, 2}$, 77^2, 87–90.
Antigonus Mattathias, 14.
Arbā'āh Ṭūrīm, 95.
'Aristeas', Letter of, 2 sq.
Arnold (*Sir* T. W.), 9^1.
Arragel (Moses). *See* Moses Arragel.
'Ārūkh (*he-*), 59.
Aubert (M.), 30^2, 49.
Augustine, *St.*, 79^1, 100^1.

Baruch, *Apocalypse of*, 47^2.
Basil, *the Macedonian*, 48^2.
Ben Asher. *See* Aaron ben Moses.
Ben Naphtali, 113.
Benveniste (Elijah ben Abraham), 109 sq.
Berliner (A.), 18.
Bēth-Alphā, synagogue at, 62–4; 107.
Bēth Ḥaghrā (or Ḥāghīrā), family of calligraphers, 6 sq.
Bevan (E.), 10^1, 16^1, 85^1, 100^1, 120^5.
Blau (L.), 4$^{2, 3}$, 61^1.
Blondheim (D. S.), 85^3.
Boaz (Joshua), 10^2.
Bonifacio Veneziano. *See* Bonifazio Veronese.
Bonifazio Veronese, 99^3.
Buchthal (H.), 42^1, 46^2, 119^3.

Castro (H. de), 11^1.
Clement of Alexandria, 85.
Cohn-Wiener (E.), 17^1, 60^2.
Cook (A. B.), 110^1.
Cook (S. A.), 14^4, 16$^{2, 4}$, 23^3, 25^3, 30^1, 77^1, 117^2, 121^2.
Cornell (H.), 120.
Coulton (G. G.), 77^1, 85^2.

Dalton (O. M.), 17^1, 30^2, 122.
Daniel, 48^1.
David ben Joseph, *Ḳimḥī*, 106, 114 sq.
Diḳdūḳē haṭ-ṭe'āmīm, 113.
Dura-Europos, synagogue at, 22 sqq.; church at, 59.

Ecclesiasticus, 20^1, 53–5.
Eisler (R.), 8^2.
Elvira, Synod of, 10.
Epistle to the Hebrews, 20^1, 63.
Epstein (J. N.), 12^1.
Eusebius, 10.
Ezekiel, 45–50.

Gabriel, *the archangel*, 48, 86^2.
Gamaliel II, 13^1.
Gaster (M.), 1, 67^2, 69^1.
Gaster (T.), 122^3.
Ginzberg (L.), 39, 44, 91^2.
God, name of, illuminated in gold and silver, 4, 5.
Goodenough (E. R.), 32–5.
Gottheil (R.), 78^3, 89^2.
Guzman (Luis de). *See* Luis de Guzman.

Ḥammām Lif, synagogue at, 65.
Higger (M.), 4.
Haphṭārōth, 51–2.
Hill (*Sir* G. F.), 14$^{3, 4}$.
Hitti (P. K.), 9^1.
Hoerning (R.), 68^4.
Holmes and Parsons, 8^1.
Holy of Holies, 14, 17.
Hopkins (C.), 45.

Ibn Ezra. *See* Abraham ben Mē'īr.
Isaac ben Solomon, *de Braga*, 114.
Isaiah, 81.
Italiener (B.), 57^1.

Jacob ben Asher, 95.
James (M. R.), 39^4, 49^2, 83^2, 94^1, 121^3.
Jellinek (A.), 27^2.
Jerash, synagogue at, 64.

GENERAL INDEX

Jerome, *St.*, 4, 10.
Jochanan bar Nappāḥā, 12, 56–7, 119.
Joseph ben Judah, *al-Ḥakīm*, 114.
Joseph Ibn Ḥayyīm, 114.
Josephus Flavius, 3, 11^1, 25^4.
Joshua ben Levi, *Amōrā*, 43.
Judah ben Samuel, *he-Ḥāsīdh*, 105.
Judah Mē'īr, *Ḳaraite*, 68^3.

Ḳaraites, 68.
Kaufmann (D.), 1, 10^2, 19, 20^1, 55, 85^3, 86^1, 87, 92^2, 93^1, ^{2}, 95^2, 96^1, 97^3, 98, 105^1, 111^1.
Kennedy (A. R. S.), 14^4.
K^{e}thubbōth, illuminated, 94.
Ḳimḥī. *See* David ben Joseph.
Kraeling (C. H.), 24, 31, 37–42^2, 44, 47 sq.
Krauss (S.), 19^1.
Künstle (K.), 122.
Kurz (O.), 61^2, 99^3.

Lamentations, 108.
Leclercq (H.), 30^1, 64^2, 100^1, 112^1.
Legrain (L.), 25.
Levy (R.), 9^1.
Lietzmann (H.), 121^1.
Luis de Guzman, 90 sq.

Maccabees (I), 7, 8.
Margoliouth (G.), 68^3, 73^1, 74$^{1, 3}$, 75$^{1, 3}$, 80^1, 81^1, 82$^{1, 2}$, 83, 113.
Mayer (A. L.), 85^4.
M^{e}ghillāh, illuminated copies of, 93.
M^{e}ghillāh (*T.B.*), 43^1.
Mē'īr ben Baruch, *of Rothenburg*, 84.
Mesnil du Buisson, *Comte du*, 30^2, 31, 33^2, 36–7, 43^2, 49, 51, 52.
Michael, *the archangel*, 48.
Michelangelo, 124^1.
Midhrāsh, 5^3, 28, 44, 121.
Midhrāsh Kōnēn, 26–7.
Midhrāsh Vay-Yiḳrā Rabbā, 81.
Mikhlōl, 114 sq.
Mī she'ānāh (s^{e}liḥāh), 19, 20^1, 55–6.
Moses Arragel, Castilian version of the Hebrew Bible, 90 sq., 94^1.
Moses Ibn Zabara, 114 sq.
Mt. Athos, manual of painting at, 39^4.
Musil (A.), 9^1.

Na'aran, synagogue at, 64.
Naḥmān bar Isaac, *Amōrā*, 26^1.
Nathan ben Jehiel, 59.
Neuss (H.), 46^2.

Omont (H.), 31^2, 64.

Panofsky (E.), 99^3.
Parchment, 8, 33^2.
Pearson (H. F.), 23.
Persius, 18^1.
Peṭīrath Ahărōn ū-Mōsheh, 91.
Philo, *Judaeus*, 3, 25^4, 40^3.
Proverbs, 25, 26.
Psalms, 24, 65^2.
Ptolemy Philadelphus, 2.
Purim, Festival of, 43, 52.

Rashī, 59^1, 75^2, 80^2, 81, 96.
Reinach (S.), 60^2.
Reinach (T.), 18^1.
Revelation, 65.
Romanoff (P.), 6^1.
Rosenau (H.), 14^4.
Rossi (G.-B. de), 17, 61^2.
Rostovtzeff (M.), 22, 23, 24, 30, 31, 32, 36^2, 37, 38, 48, 56–8, 59, 123.

Samaritans, 65^1, 66–7.
Samuel ben Samuel Ibn Mūsā, 114.
Saxl (F.), 122^3.
Scribes. *See Sōphēr*.
Shabbāth (*T.B.*), 3.
Simon, *Maccabaeus*, 14.
Sloane (J. C.), 14^4.
Solomon ben Raphael, 107.
Sōph^{e}rīm (I), 4, 5; (II), 4.
Strzygowski (J.), 14^4, 29, 120.
Sukenik (E. L.), 10^1, 17^3, 34^2, 48, 62.
Sukkāh (*T.B.*), 77.
Swete (H. B.), 3.
Synagogues. *See* Bēth-Alphā; Dura-Europos; Ḥammām Lif; Jerash; Na'aran.

Ta'ănīth (*T.B.*), 25–6.
Temple, 11^1, 16^1, 25.
Tertullian, 10.
Texeira (R. S.), 11^1.
Thackeray (H. St. J.), 3^1.
Thompson (*Sir* E. M.), 4^1.

Vellum. *See* Parchment.

Walīd I, II, 9^1.
Wischnitzer-Bernstein (R.), 1, 16^4, 78^1, 117^2.
Wodtke (G.), 46^2, 119^2.
Wulff (O.), 120.

Yehoshua, son of Asayahu, 117^1.
Yōmā (*T.B.*), 11^1, 77, 84^1.

INDEX II

TYPES, SYMBOLS, AND OTHER SUBJECTS OF ILLUSTRATION

The following abbreviations are employed: *c* (coins), *f* (fresco), *g* (gold glass), *m* (mosaic), *mi* (miniature or illumination), *s* (sculpture).

Aaron. See also High Priest.
Aaron and the Urim and Thummim, *mi*, 79–80 (14); before the altar, *mi*, 89; burning incense on the Golden Altar, *mi*, 76 (12); pouring oil into the lamps of the M^{e}nōrāh, *mi*, 74 (1), 79 (13), 88.
Abraham entertaining the angels, *mi*, 74 (5); 100; frightening the birds from the sacrifice, *f*, 45(?).
Adam naming the animals, *mi*, 99; and Eve, *f*, 59; chased out of Paradise, *mi*, 86 (2); and the Serpent, *mi*, 78 (9); 86 (1); 95; 99.
Ahasuerus and the angel Gabriel, *mi*, 91; extending his sceptre to Esther, *mi*, 76 (3); 88; seated, with sceptre, *mi*, 90.
Angel announcing the birth of a son to Abraham, *mi*, 75 (6).
Angel of Death bringing Sarah to Mount Moriah, *mi*, 88.
Ark of the Covenant (*Ārōn hab-b^{e}rīth*), *mi*, 63, 64, 67, 79.
Ark of the Law. See Tōrāh shrine.
Armed knight on horseback, *mi*, 89.

Balaam and his ass, *mi*, 87 (46).
Bar-Yokhnī (fabulous bird), *mi*, 77 (3).
Behemoth, *m*, 65.
Bondage of the Israelites in Egypt, *mi*, 86 (32–3); 103.
Brazen Serpent, *mi*, 76 (10); 82 (5); 87 (45).
Bunch of grapes brought back from the Holy Land, *mi*, 87 (44).

Cain slaying Abel, *mi*, 86 (3), 99.
Cain and Abel bringing their offerings, *mi*, 99.
Canaan, maps of, 96.
Cherubim over the Mercy Seat, 111 (painted in Second Temple, not carved); drawing of, 67; *mi*, 79 (12); 92; 107.
censer, *mi*, 79 (12).
Circumcision of Isaac, *mi*, 88.

Daniel in the lions' den, *m*, 64; *mi*, 76 (2); 98; seated, with the golden vessels, *mi*, 90.
David, *mi*, 115, 116; anointed by Samuel, 41; playing on the lyre (or harp), *f*, 29 sq.; *mi*, 74 (4); 90; 93; 98; surprising Saul asleep, *f*, 45; tended by Bathsheba and the Shunammite woman, *mi*, 89.
David and Goliath, *f*, 59; *mi*, 80 (15); 97.
Destruction of Sodom and Gomorra, *mi*, 75 (7), 81 (1?); 101.
Discovery of the Infant Moses. See Moses rescued from the Nile.
Drowning of the Egyptians in the Red Sea, *f*, 36; *mi*, 86 (41); 104.

Egyptian smiting the Israelite, *mi*, 102.
Elijah and the Prophets of Baal, *f*, 44; and the Widow's Cruse (?), *f*, 44; reviving the Widow's Son, *f*, 43; riding an ass and proclaiming the coming of the Messiah, *mi*, 97; sacrificing on Mount Carmel, *f*, 44.
Elkanah offering up a lamb, *mi*, 89.
Esau returning from the chase, *mi*, 86 (10); 101.
Esther assembling her compatriots and proclaiming a three-day fast, *mi*, 98; pleading before Ahasuerus, *mi*, 80 (16); and Mordecai, *f*, 42 sq. See also Ahasuerus.
ethrōgh, *c*, 14; *g*, 17; on catacombs, 19; *m*, 23, 63.
Eve emerging from the rib of Adam, *mi*, 99.
Exiles in Babylon hanging up their harps, *mi*, 93.
Exodus, the, *f*, 35; *mi*, 86 (39); 89. See also Israelites crossing the Red Sea.
Ezekiel, visions of, *f*, 45 sqq. (Valley of the Dry Bones); *mi*, 90 ('Four Living Creatures').
Ezra, *mi*, 90.

TYPES, SYMBOLS, AND OTHER SUBJECTS 139

fish, g, 18.
'Fountain of Life', m, 65.

Gan 'Ēdhen (Paradise), 26–7, 65.
God, depiction of, 11¹, 100¹.

Hanging of Haman and his ten sons, mi, 88; 93²; 98.
ḥăṣōṣᵉrōth (silver trumpets), c and s, 15; drawing of, 67.
High Priest (Aaron?) sacrificing, f, 37 sq.
Holy of Holies, c, 14⁴; f, 23.
Hosea speaking to women, mi, 90.

Isaac blessing Jacob, mi, 86 (9), 101. See also Sacrifice of Isaac.
Isaiah exhorting the Israelites, mi, 89.
Israelites entering Pithom and Rameses, mi, 89; gathering manna, mi, 89; kneeling and praying, mi, 89; crossing the Red Sea, f, 35 sq.; mi, 75 (9); 82 (3); 86 (40); 98; 104; taking with them the bones of Joseph, mi, 89.

Jacob blessing Ephraim and Manasseh, f, 30; mi, 102; blessing his sons, f, 30; blessing Pharaoh, mi, 102; crossing the Jabbok, mi, 101; mourning for Joseph, mi, 101; wrestling with the angel, mi, 86 (12); 101; dream of, f, 45 (?); mi, 86 (11); 101; ladder of, in figured Māsōrāh, 109; death of, mi, 102. See also Tents of Jacob and his wives.
Jeremiah exhorting the Israelites, mi, 89.
Jerusalem, walls of, mi, 90.
Job, tribulation of, mi, 88; restored to prosperity, mi, 98.
Jonah and the whale, m, 61 (?); mi, 83; 115, 116.
Joseph and his brethren in Egypt, mi, 86 (25–31); 102; fleeing from Potiphar's wife, mi, 86 (19); 95; 101; interpreting the dreams of Pharaoh's butler and baker, mi, 86 (20–1); 101; interpreting Pharaoh's dreams, mi, 86 (23); 102; meeting 'a certain man', mi, 86 (15); 101; sold to the Ishmaelites, mi, 86 (18); 101; stripped of his coat, mi, 86 (17); 101; dreams of, mi, 86 (13–14); 101; triumph of, mi, 86 (24).
Joseph's brethren tending their flocks, mi, 86 (16); plotting to kill Joseph, mi, 101; bringing Joseph's coat to Jacob, mi, 101.
Joshua and the Angel, f, 34; mi, 97; bidding the sun to stand still, f, 34; receives the magic staff from God, mi, 89.
Judgement of Solomon. See Solomon.
Judgement upon the sinners in Hell (?), mi, 81 (1).
Judith slaying Holofernes, mi, 76 (11).

Leviathan, m, 65; mi, 77 (5).
lion, s, 10–11.
Lot and his family escaping from the city of Sodom, 75 (8); 81 (2); 101; wife of, turned into a pillar of salt, mi, 75 (8); 81 (2); daughters of, in the cave, mi, 75 (8).
lūlābh, c, 14; g, 17; f, 23; m, 63; on catacombs, 19.

Māghēn Dāvīdh (hexagram), mi, 71, 116, 117.
manna, jar of, mi, 107, 112.
Maze of Jericho, mi, 110.
Mᵉnōrāh, c, 14; on Arch of Titus, 15; on catacombs, 16; g, 17, 18; m, 23, 66; drawing of, 67; mi, 74 (1); 88; 107, 111.
Mercy Seat. See Cherubim over the Mercy Seat.
Messianic Life. See Gan 'Ēdhen.
Miriam and the women of Israel celebrating the triumph over the Egyptians, mi, 87 (42); 89; 104.
Moses and the burning bush, f, 32 sq.; mi, 86 (36–7); 102; before Pharaoh, mi, 89; dividing the Red Sea, mi, 75 (9); 82 (3); 83; expounding the Law, f, 32 sq.; 95 (to the Israelites); praying for victory, mi, 80 (17); being rescued from the Nile, f, 41; mi, 86 (34–5); 102; rescuing the daughters of Reuel (Jethro) from the shepherds, mi, 102; (Solomon?) reading the Law, mi, 74 (3); speaking to a group of Israelites, mi, 89; slaying the Egyptian, mi, 102; striking the Rock, mi, 75 (10); 82 (6); death of, mi, 91. See also Israelites crossing the Red Sea; Revelation of the Law.
Moses and Aaron before Pharaoh, f, 31 (?); mi, 86 (38); 103; performing miracles before the Israelites, mi, 103.

INDEX II

Moses and his family returning to Egypt, *mi*, 103.
Mount of Olives, *mi*, 112.
Musical instruments of the Levites, *mi*, 111.

Nebuchadnezzar calling upon the three youths to worship the golden image, *mi*, 76 (1).
Nimrod ordering Abraham to be cast into the fiery furnace, *mi*, 100.
Noah being carried out drunk from his tent, *mi*, 100; planting a vine, *mi*, 86 (5); 100.
Noah's Ark, *m*, 64; *mi*, 79 (10); 86 (4); 99, 112.

oil vessel, on catacombs, 19.
'Orpheus mosaic', 29–30.
ostrich, *m*, 63.

Palmistry, miniature depicting, 74 (2).
Paradise. See Gan 'Ēdhen.
pārōkheth, *c*, 14; *mi*, 64.
peacocks, *m*, 65.
Pharaoh pursuing the Israelites, *mi*, 89, 104; upbraiding the Jewish midwives, *f*, 41; *mi*, 102; dreams of, *mi*, 86 (22); 102. See also Israelites crossing the Red Sea.
Phinehas, with lance and shield, *mi*, 115, 116; slaying Zimri, *mi*, 91.
Preparation of the Passover, *mi*, 104.

Revelation of the Law on Mount Sinai, *mi*, 87 (43); 88; 92; 94; 97.
rods, flowering and barren, *m*, 63; drawing of, 68; *mi*, 78 (7); 82 (4); 107, 112.
Ruth amongst the reapers, *mi*, 94; spinning, *mi*, 90.

Sacrifice of Isaac, *f*, 23; *m*, 62; *mi*, 79 (11); 86 (8); 88; 95; 101; in figured Māsōrāh, 109.
Samson pulling down the palace of the Philistines, *mi*, 97; rending the lion, *mi*, 77 (8); 97.
'Samson and Delila mosaic', 60, 118.
Samuel slaying Agag, *mi*, 80 (18); 97²; the infant Samuel being presented to Eli, *mi*, 97. See also David anointed by Samuel.
Sarah listening at the tent, 75 (6). See also Angel of Death.

Satan falling from the skies, *mi*, 90; in the presence of God (?), *mi*, 90.
Saul in flight, *mi*, 93.
Scribe at work, *mi*, 90.
Sea in Temple of Solomon, *mi*, 76 (12).
Shield of David. See *Māghēn Dāvīdh*.
Sisera being pursued by the archers, *mi*, 98.
shōphār, *c*, 18; on catacombs, 19; *m*, 63.
Shōr hab-bār, *mi*, 77 (6).
snuff-dishes, *m*, 63.
Solomon expounding wisdom, *mi*, 90; reading the Law (?), *mi*, 74 (3); seated on his throne, *mi*, 98; Judgement of, *f*, 60 sq.; 118; *mi*, 77 (4); 97.
stags, *m*, 65.
Sun, moon, and stars, *mi*, 77 (2).

Tabernacle, 14⁴; *f*, 39; *mi*, 89; vessels of, *mi*, 88; drawings of, 96.
Table of the Shewbread, *s*, 15; drawing of, 67; *mi*, 79 (12), 107, 111.
Tables of the Law, *mi*, 107, 112. See also Revelation of the Law.
Temple, *f*, 37, 38; Service of the Temple, *mi*, 92.
Ten Commandments, miniatures illustrating, 95.
Ten plagues, *mi*, 89; 103–4.
Tents of Jacob and his wives, *mi*, 109 sq.
Three Youths in the fiery furnace, *mi*, 76 (1).
Tongs and fire-pans, *mi*, 107.
Tōrāh shrine (*Ārōn haḳ-ḳōdhesh*), 14⁴; *g*, 17–19; *m*, 63.
Tower of Babel, *mi*, 86 (6–7).
'Tree of Knowledge', *m*, 65.
'Tree of Life', *m*, 24 sqq., 65.
Triumph of Mordecai, *mi*, 80 (19); 88. See also Esther and Mordecai.

Urim and Thummim, *mi*, 112. See also Aaron.

Vashti, and the archangel Gabriel, *mi*, 92.
Vine, *f*, 24; in Herod's Temple, 25.
Visions of Ezekiel. See Ezekiel.

Wells of Elim, *f*, 39 sq.; *mi*, 39 sq.

Zodiac, Signs of, *mi*, 76 (1; third series).

INDEX III

OBJECTS DESCRIBED OR DISCUSSED

BERLIN. *Kaiser-Friedrich-Museum.*
Gold glass, 17–18.
BĒTH-ALPHĀ.
Mosaic in ancient synagogue, 62 sq.
CAIRO. *Egyptian Synagogue.*
Hebrew Bible (now lost), 89 sq.
CAMBRIDGE. *University Library.*
Copy of the Hagiographa (Schiller-Szinessy 25), 89[1].
— *Trinity College Library.*
Hebrew Bible (G. 1), 108.
CRACOW. *Library of the Jewish Community.*
Hebrew Bible, 87 sq.
DAMASCUS. *New Museum.*
Frescoes of the synagogue at Dura-Europos, 22 sqq.; of the chapel, 59.
JERUSALEM. *Schocken Library.*
Hebrew Pentateuch, &c., 86 sq.
ḤAMMĀM LIF.
Mosaic, 65.
ḲUṢAIR 'AMRAH.
Wall-paintings, 9[1].
LEMBERG.
Hebrew Bible, 90.
LENINGRAD. *State Library.*
Hebrew Bibles, 67 sq.
LONDON. *British Museum.*
Coins, 14–15.
Glass-disk, 19. 50.
Mosaic from Carthage, 65.
Hebrew Bibles (including portions thereof), Add. 9405, 108[1]; Add. 15282, 107 sq.; Or. 1467, 71; Or. 2363, 70; Or. 2626–8 (Lisbon Bible), 113 sq.
Hebrew Bible and *Maḥăzōr*, Add. 11639, 72 sq.
Maḥăzōr, Add. 22413, 94 sq.
Haggādhāh, Or. 2737, 97; Add. 27210, 99 sq.
Arbā'āh Ṭūrīm, Harleian 5717, 95.
— *Lambeth Palace Library.*
Latin Bible (no. 3), 49 sq., 99[3].

— *Sassoon Library.*
Farḥī Bible (no. 368), 109 sq.
De Castro Bible (no. 506), 108[1].
MADRID. *Casa de Alba.*
Castilian version of the Hebrew Bible, 90 sq.
MALTA.
'Samson and Delila' mosaic, 60.
NABLŪS. *Samaritan Synagogue.*
Metal case of *Sēpher Tōrāh*, 67 sq.
NEW YORK. *Library of J. Pierpont Morgan.*
French MS. of O.T. illustrations, 83[2].
— *Library of the Jewish Theological Seminary.*
Maḥăzōr, 95.
NUREMBERG. *German National Museum.*
Second *Haggādhāh*, 40, 97.
OXFORD. *Bodleian Library.*
Hebrew Bible (Kennicott 1), 114 sq.
PARIS. *Bibliothèque Nationale.*
Hebrew Bible (no. 7), 106 sq.
Gregory Nazianzenus (Gr. 510), 42, 46, 48[2], 50, 119.
— *Rothschild Library.*
Siddūr, 97 sq.
PARMA. *De Rossi Library.*
Hebrew Psalter (no. 510), 93.
Biblical commentaries (no. 878), 95.
POMPEII.
Paintings caricaturing Jewish themes (?), 61.
ROME.
Arch of Titus, 15.
Catacombs, 5, 16, 18, 19.
— *Museo Borgiano.*
Gold glass, 18.
— *Vatican.*
Gold glass, 17.
SARAJEVO. *Museum.*
Haggādhāh, 37 sq., 98 sq.

INDEX IV

GLOSSARY OF HEBREW AND ARAMAIC TERMS

Āmōrā, a teacher of the Law (*Hălăkhāh*), who lived after the compilation of the Mishnāh but before the redaction of the two Talmūdhs.

Ărōn hab-b^{e}rīth, Ark of the Covenant.

Ărōn hak-kōdhesh, Torah shrine.

Bāraithā, a pronouncement by a Tannā, but one not forming part of the *Mishnāh*.

ethrōgh, citron.

Haphṭārāh, pl. *Haphṭārōth*, readings from the Prophets.

Haggādhāh, pl. *Haggādhōth*, the service of the Passover.

ḥăṣōṣ^{e}rōth, silver trumpets.

ḥazzān, cantor.

kathbānīm ummānīm, artistic scribes.

lūlābh, palm-branch.

Maḥăzōr, the service for the Holy Days and the Festivals.

Māsōrāh, corpus of textual notes on the Hebrew Bible.

M^{e}nōrāh, golden candlestick.

Mūsāph, additional service (in the liturgy).

parashiyyōth, pericopes (of the Pentateuch).

pārōkheth, curtain before the Holy of Holies.

piyyūṭ, a liturgical poem.

s^{e}līḥāh, a prayer asking for forgiveness.

Sēpher Tōrāh, scroll of the Law.

Shābhū'ōth, Pentecost.

shōphār, ram's horn.

Siddūr, the Daily Prayers; used amongst the Spanish and Portuguese Jews also for the Service of the Holy Days and Festivals.

sōphēr (pl. *sōph^{e}rīm*), scribe.

Sukkōth, Festival of Tabernacles.

tāghīn, crowns (on certain letters).

Tannā, a teacher of the Law (*Hălăkhāh*), whose pronouncements are recorded in the *Mishnāh* and *Bāraithās*.

Targūm, Aramaic version of the Hebrew Bible.

ṭallīth, praying-shawl.

Yōm Kippūr, Day of Atonement.

PLATES

PLATE I

1

2

3

4

1-4. Coins

5. Arch of Titus

PLATE II

1

2

3

1–3. Gold Glass

Jewish Catacomb on the Via Montana, Rome

PLATE IV

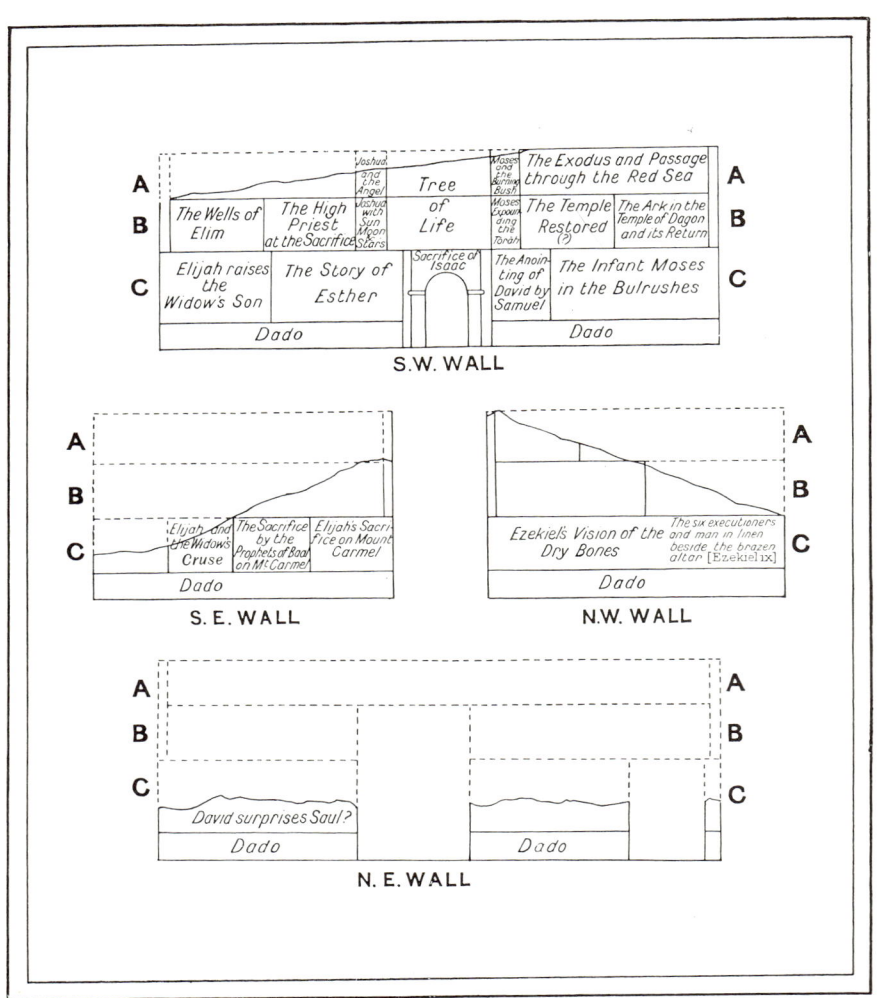

Plan of the Synagogue Frescoes, Dura-Europos

PLATE V

1. Sacrifice of Isaac, &c., Dura-Europos

2. Sacrifice of Isaac, Hebrew Bible, Ambrosian Library

PLATE VI

1. David playing upon the Lyre, &c., Dura-Europos

2. 'Orpheus Mosaic', Jerusalem

PLATE VII

1. Moses and the Burning Bush, Dura-Europos

2. Moses expounding the Law, Dura-Europos

PLATE VIII

1. Joshua and the Angel, Dura-Europos

2. Joshua orders the Sun to stay his Course, Dura-Europos

PLATE IX

1. The Restored Temple (?), Dura-Europos

2. The Restored Temple, Sarajevo Haggādhāh

PLATE X

High Priest at the Sacrifice, Dura-Europos

PLATE XI

1. Wells of Elim (?), Dura-Europos

2. Wells of Elim, Sarajevo Haggādhāh

PLATE XII

1. Exodus and Passage of the Israelites through the Red Sea, Dura-Europos

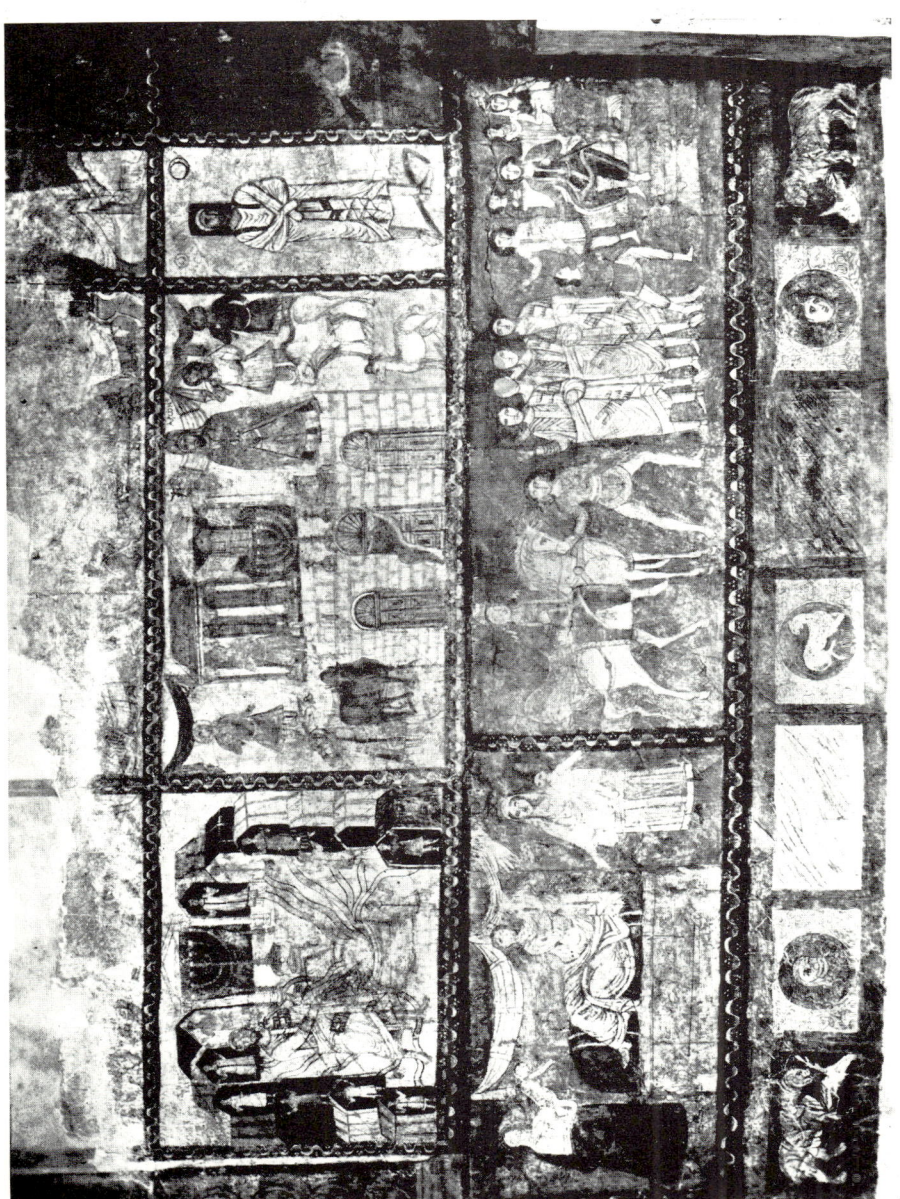

Elijah and the Widow's Son and the Story of Esther (Register C), Dura-Europos

PLATE XIV

Vision of Ezekiel (Register C), Dura-Europos

PLATE XV

1 (No. 2). Vision of Ezekiel, Gold Glass, British Museum (cf. Plate XIV)

2. Vision of Ezekiel, Gregory Nazianzenus, Gr. 510, Bibliothèque Nationale (cf. Plate XIV)

PLATE XVI

1. Vision of Ezekiel, Latin Bible (no. 3), Lambeth (cf. Plate XIV)

2. Vision of Ezekiel, Castilian Bible, Casa de Alba, Madrid (cf. Plate XIV)

PLATE XVII

'Samson and Delilah' mosaic, Malta

PLATE XVIII

Synagogue mosaic at Bēth-Ālphā

PLATE XIX

1. Ark of the Covenant?
Syriac MS. (no. 341), Bibliothèque Nationale

2. Ark of the Covenant?
Ashburnham Pentateuch, Bibliothèque Nationale

1. Paradisal scene, Synagogue mosaic, Ḥammām Līf

2. Paradisal Scene (?), mosaic from Carthage, British Museum

PLATE XXI

Vessels of the Tabernacle, Pentateuch, 930 A.D., Leningrad

PLATE XXII

Vessels of the Tabernacle, Case of Samaritan Scroll, Gaster Collection

PLATE XXIII

1. Fragment of figured Māsōrāh, Hebrew Bible, Leningrad

2. Frontispiece, Book of Exodus, Ḳaraïte MS., Or. 2540, British Museum

PLATE XXIV

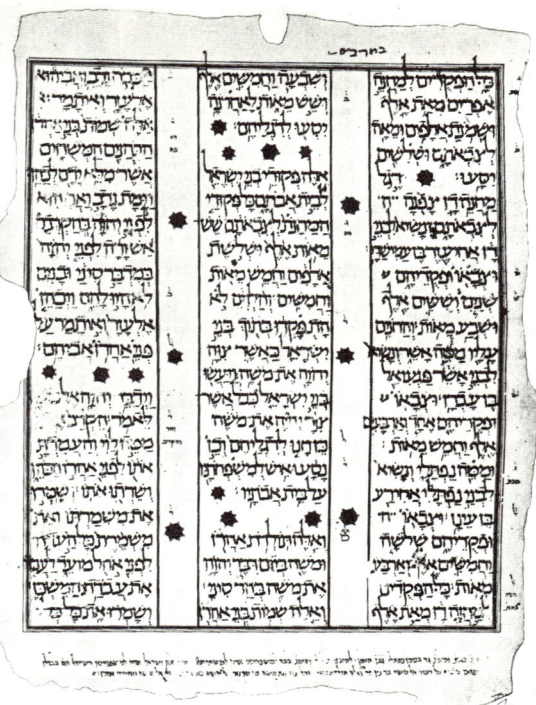

1. Page from an illuminated Hebrew Bible,
Or. 9879, British Museum

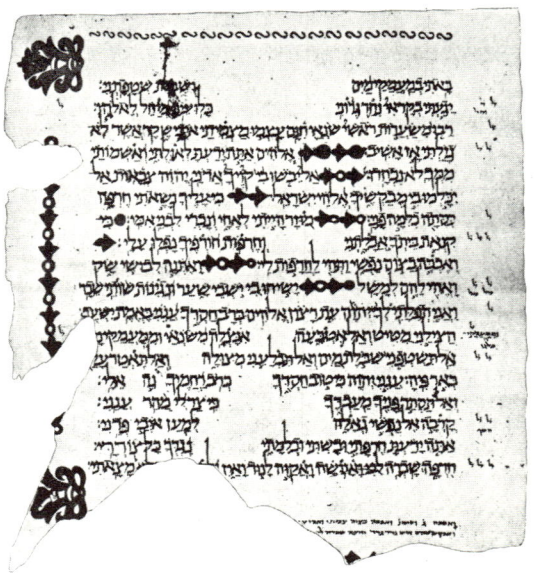

2. Page from an illuminated Hebrew Bible,
Or. 9880, British Museum

PLATE XXV

1. Aaron lighting the Menōrāh, Add. 11639, British Museum

2. The Sacrifice of Isaac, Add. 11639

PLATE XXVI

1. The Angels destroying the cities of Sodom and Gomorra, Add. 11639

2. The Cherubim over the Mercy Seat, Add. 11639

PLATE XXVII

1. The High Priest and the Urim and Thummim, Add. 11639

2. The Triumph of Mordecai, Add. 11639

PLATE XXVIII

1. The Destruction of Sodom (?), Add. 11639

2. Moses cleaving the Red Sea with his Rod, Add. 11639

PLATE XXIX

Frontispiece, Hebrew Pentateuch, &c., Salman (Schocken) Library, Jerusalem

PLATE XXX

1. Death of Moses, Alba Bible

2. Story of Esther, Alba Bible

PLATE XXXI

1

2

1-2. Miniatures from Haggādhāh, Add. 27210, British Museum

PLATE XXXII

1

2

1-2. Miniatures from Haggādhāh,
Add. 27210

PLATE XXXIII

Frontispiece to Book of Numbers,
Add. 15282, British Museum

PLATE XXXIV

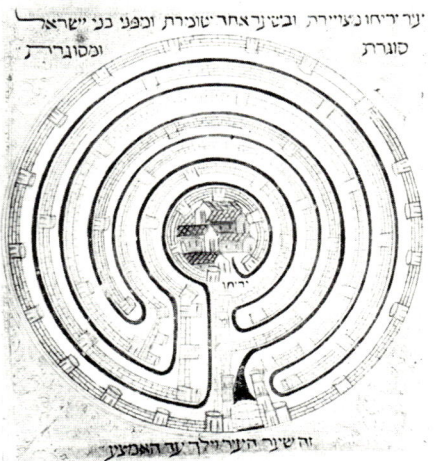

1. Maze leading to (and from) Jericho,
   Farḥī Bible

2. Tents of Jacob and his wives,
   Farḥī Bible

PLATE XXXV

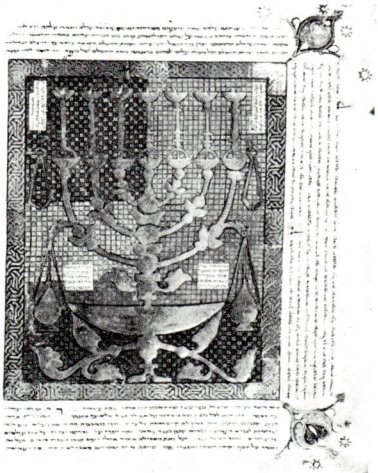

1. The Menōrāh, Farḥī Bible

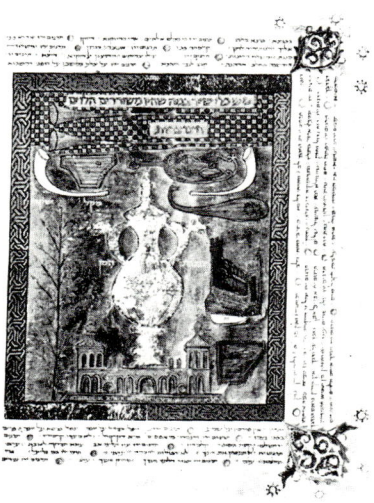

2. Musical instruments of the Levites, Farḥī Bible

PLATE XXXVI

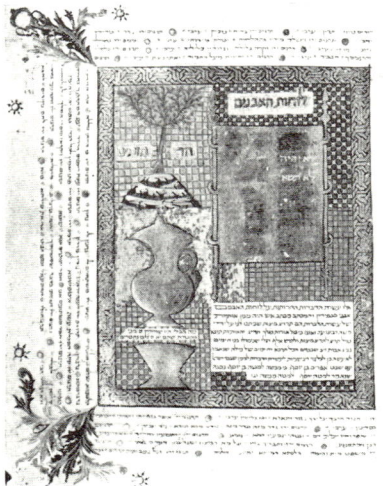

1. Tables of the Law, &c.,
Farḥī Bible

2. Arabesque, Farḥī Bible

Page from Lisbon Bible, Or. 2626, British Museum

PLATE XXXVIII

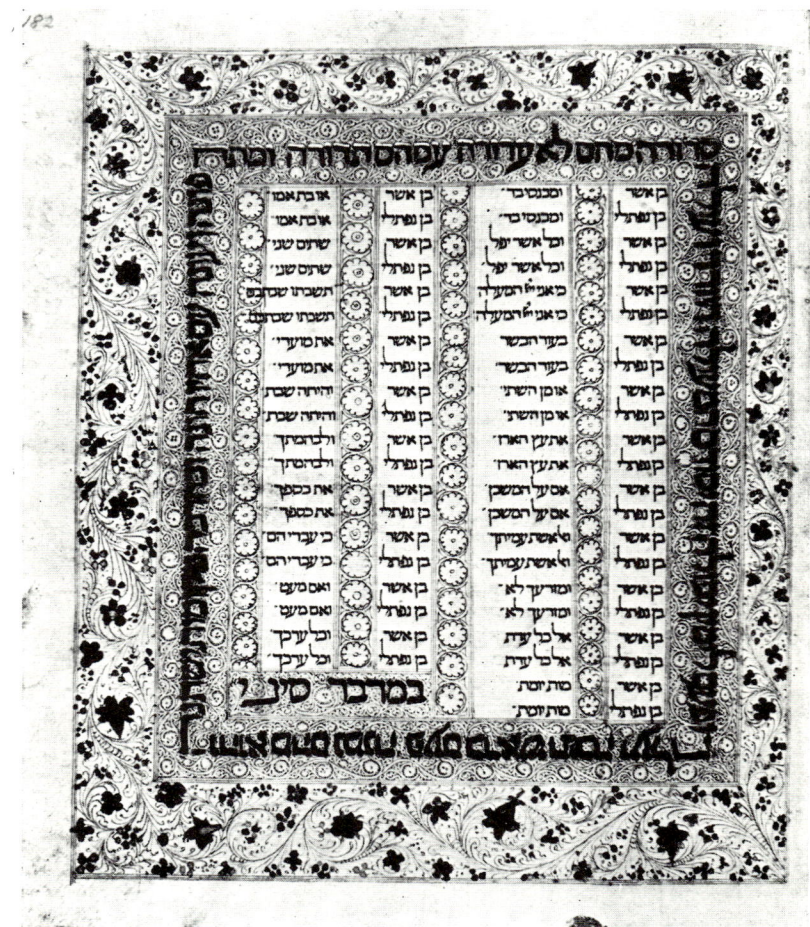

Another page from the Lisbon Bible, Or. 2626, British Museum

PLATE XXXIX

1. Page from Kennicott Bible, Bodleian Library

2. Beginning of Genesis, Kennicott Bible

PLATE XL

1. King David, Kennicott Bible, Bodleian Library

2. Jonah and the Whale, Kennicott Bible

PLATE XLI

1. 'Shield of David', Kennicott Bible

2. Arabesque, Kennicott Bible, Bodleian Library